THE FIRST DAY OF THE NEW CREATION

THE FIRST DAY OF THE NEW CREATION

The Resurrection and the Christian Faith

by

VESELIN KESICH

ST. VLADIMIR'S SEMINARY PRESS
CRESTWOOD, NEW YORK 10707
1982

Library of Congress Cataloging in Publication Data
Kesich, Veselin, 1921-
   The first day of the new creation.

   Bibliography: p.
   Includes index.
   1. Jesus Christ—Resurrection.
2. Resurrection.   I. Title.
BT481.K42   232'.5   81-21516
ISBN 0-913836-78-8   AACR2

© Copyright 1982

by

ST. VLADIMIR'S SEMINARY PRESS

ISBN 0-913836-78-8

PRINTED IN THE UNITED STATES OF AMERICA
BY
ATHENS PRINTING COMPANY

Preface

No study can do complete justice to the theme of resurrection with all its complexity and ramifications. I am indebted to many scholars and interpreters, from whom I have learned and to whom I express my gratitude, and I trust I have faithfully conveyed their points of view. For any misunderstandings of their positions I bear full responsibility. This study is based upon the conviction and witness of the New Testament that the rise of the Christian faith is rooted in the death and resurrection of Christ. If the reader is prompted to go back to the New Testament sources, I would be gratified.

I am grateful to St. Vladimir's Seminary Press for publishing this book, to David Drillock and Theodore Bazil for their interest and for not letting me forget that I had to finish it, and to Paul Kachur, my editor at the press, for his cooperation, suggestions, and for providing the translation of St John Chrysostom's Easter homily. Stephen Beskid of the seminary library has been of invaluable assistance, providing materials necessary for this study. I also owe much to my students; many of the questions discussed here were raised by them.

I am particularly grateful to my wife Lydia, without whose help in the preparation of the manuscript this book would not have been completed. When I read in acknowledgments about the valuable services that the wives of certain authors have performed, I used to think that they might be exaggerating a little. Now I know that what they write is true.

St. Vladimir's Seminary
Crestwood, N.Y.
Feast of the Annunciation, 1981

Contents

A section of icon plates is included between pages 96 and 97.

". . . if Christ has not been raised, then our preaching is in vain and your faith is in vain."

1 Corinthians 15:14

Come, one and all, and receive the banquet of faith!
Come, one and all, and receive the riches of lovingkindness!
No one must lament his poverty,
    for a kingdom belonging to all has appeared;
no one must despair over his failings,
    for forgiveness has sprung up from the grave;
no one must fear death,
    for the death of the Savior has set us all free.

Easter Homily of St John Chrysostom

Introduction

Many Christians are confronted with enormous difficulties over how to understand the New Testament teaching of the resurrection. What does it mean when we say "Christ is risen"? What is the meaning of the bodily resurrection, and how was it understood in the primitive Church of the New Testament times as well as in the Church of the early fathers? Was the belief in resurrection shaped by what is given in the Old Testament and early Judaism—a product of the Hebrew mind—or does it stand by itself as something completely new? Was the gospel account of the resurrection influenced by mystery cults of dying and rising gods? Is resurrection of the body the same as resuscitation of the body or physical restoration of life, as some literalists would insist? These and many other questions and comments have been raised in ordinary conversations, in scholarly debates and at various religious gatherings. They have been the stimulus for writing this book.

The origin of Christianity is different from the beginnings of any other religious movement in the history of religions. Christianity appeared as a community, as the Church, which arose with the death and resurrection of Jesus Christ. What distinguishes the early Christians from those who followed Judaism or the religions and cults of the Hellenistic age was primarily their conviction about Jesus and his resurrection and their personal relationship with the risen Christ. The message of resurrection is the center of the New Testament, which is justifiably called the book of the Church. It would never have been written without the faith of the early Christians in the resurrected Christ. As Nicholas Arseniev has observed, the New

Testament resurrection narratives are "permeated by the sense of the overpowering Presence of the Risen One."[1]

All our sources for the resurrection of Christ are of Christian origin. There could not be non-Christian witnesses to the resurrection, for those to whom Christ appeared after his resurrection became his followers and witnesses.

The letters of St Paul are our earliest written documents permeated with the faith in the risen Christ. The earliest record of the resurrection tradition we have is the list of appearances that Paul received from the primitive Church and incorporated and handed down in 1 Corinthians 15:3-8:

> For I delivered to you as of first importance what I also received, that Christ died for our sins in accordance with the scriptures, that he was buried, that he was raised on the third day in accordance with the scriptures, and that he appeared to Cephas, then to the twelve. Then he appeared to more than five hundred brethren at one time, most of whom are still alive, though some have fallen asleep. Then he appeared to James, then to all the apostles. Last of all, as to one untimely born, he appeared also to me.

This is a summary of primitive Christian preaching about the resurrection, what is known as the "kerygma." We shall be referring to this passage, discussing and analyzing it, throughout this book. Scholarship attests that this is one of the earliest Christian documents, possibly composed within ten years of the death of Jesus. And we may assume that even earlier St Paul could have learned of the appearance of the risen Christ to Peter and James when he visited these leaders themselves after his conversion (Ga 1:18-19).

Although the gospels were written in the second half of the first century, after the epistles of Paul, their narratives of the resurrection incorporate old and original material from oral

[1]Nicholas Arseniev, *Revelation of Life Eternal: An Introduction to the Christian Message*, Orthodox Theological Library, 2 (New York: SVS Press, n.d.) 78.

tradition. They preserved the memory of what had happened on the morning of the first Easter Sunday. St Paul does not mention the women and their discovery of the empty tomb, for instance, whereas all four evangelists give accounts of this event. The gospels stress the importance of the empty tomb, which St Paul does not mention. As we shall see below, however, he was not ignorant of it.

In addition to 1 Corinthians 15 and the resurrection accounts that come at the end of each of the gospels, we shall also take into account the apostolic preaching in the book of Acts, particularly the speech of St Peter on the day of Pentecost and the narratives of Paul's conversion.

Our sources testify to the empty tomb, the appearances of the risen Christ and the power of the Spirit. There is no witness to the actual moment of the resurrection itself and no attempt to narrate that event. Still, the details of subsequent events, such as the reactions of the witnesses to the empty tomb and the appearances of the risen Christ, prove that faith in him was not the product of theological reflection but came from what was seen and heard. The gospels transmit the experience of those witnesses to us, so that we are able to relive them.

The liturgical texts and hymns used in the Holy Week and Easter services of the Orthodox Church as well as her iconography make these events present again for us. We shall draw on them to indicate how the resurrection faith has been lived in the tradition of the Church. We shall also refer to the writings of the fathers of the Church, who lived close to the time and spirit of the New Testament and whose theology springs from meditation upon the Bible.

In addition, no book on the resurrection today should be written without a certain amount of the knowledge and insight of contemporary New Testament research. The works of modern exegetes are used in our discussion in connection with a variety of problems of a historical and exegetical character, illuminating our understanding of the tradition.

1

The Question of Resurrection

For the members of the first Christian community in Jerusalem, the resurrection of Christ was above all an event in the life of their Master, and then also in their own lives. After meeting Christ following his resurrection, they could have said with St Paul that necessity was laid upon them to preach the gospel of resurrection (1 Cor 9:16). Christianity spread throughout the Greco-Roman world with the proclamation that Jesus who died on the cross was raised to a new life by God. The message of Christianity is without parallel in religious history in its content and in its demand: "Repent, and be baptized every one of you in the name of Jesus Christ for the forgiveness of your sins; and you shall receive the gift of the Holy Spirit" (Acts 2:38). C.F.D. Moule, a well-known British New Testament scholar, has noted that although there is much in Christianity that would be congenial to members of many other religions, "yet the elements in the New Testament which a non-Christian would not share," that is, the belief in "Jesus as crucified and raised from among the dead, and of man's relationship to God through him," are "precisely the ones which alone account for the Church's existence."[1]

When Muhammad died at the age of sixty-two, his followers had great difficulty in accepting it as a fact, as the end of Muhammad's life—they could not be reconciled with it. Then the second caliph, Umar, proclaimed: "By God he is not dead:

[1]C. F. D. Moule, *The Phenomenon of the New Testament: An Inquiry into the Implications of Certain Features of the New Testament,* Studies in Biblical Theology, 2d series, 1 (London: SCM Press, 1967) 15.

15

he has gone to his Lord as Moses went and was hidden from his people for forty days, returning to them after it was said that he had died. By God, the apostle will return as Moses returned." He was immediately corrected by Abu Bakr, the first caliph, who was particularly devoted to his teacher and prophet and said: "O men, if anyone worships Muhammad, Muhammad is dead: if anyone worships God, God is alive, immortal," denying any resurrection of the prophet.[2]

The Church actually rests upon well-defined historical events, upon the historical person of Christ and his work, rather than upon promulgated doctrines.[3] This man Jesus alone was raised up in glory. His resurrection is not a myth expressing man's longing for a life of endless duration, but the fulfilment of God's design for man's salvation. In his discussion of the resurrection in 1 Corinthians 15, St Paul combined two kinds of evidence, one historical and the other the experience of this past event. In 15:3ff he enumerates historical facts, and in 15:14 and 17 he refers to the present faith: "if Christ has not been raised, then our preaching is in vain and your faith is in vain . . . your faith is futile and you are still in your sins." Faith depends on what happened in the past. The event on which it is grounded and from which it is fed did happen. Faith is organically linked with the facts, and these facts themselves determine the manner of interpretation, that is, the meaning the disciples ascribe to and derive from Christ's resurrection.

It has never been easy to express the meaning of the resurrection. The terms used to signify what actually happened can never be perfect. We speak about the resurrection of Lazarus and the resurrection of Christ—the terminology is the same, yet only in the context of the appearances of Christ after his

[2]See Geoffrey Parrinder, *Avatar and Incarnation: The Wilde Lectures in Natural and Comparative Religion in the University of Oxford* (New York: Barnes and Noble, 1970) 217-8.

[3]The Church rests upon "divine redemption *from within* history," which was brought about by the "wrenching of one man's flesh and spilling of His blood upon one particular square yard of ground, outside one particular city gate during three particular unrepeatable hours, which could have been measured on a clock," writes Gregory Dix in his stimulating book *Jew and Greek* (Glasgow: University Press, 1977) 5.

resurrection do we know that it is different from the resurrection of Lazarus. The term "resurrection" is primarily determined by what happened to Christ, and then by the change that took place in the disciples. Christ comes first. The experience of salvation is defined in reference to him.

Developments in Modern Scholarship

Biblical scholars have developed sophisticated methods for the literary and historical investigation of biblical texts. Their studies no longer ignore the community within which these documents appeared, but take the faith and needs of the Christian Church seriously into account. Modern scholars predominantly recognize that the needs of the early Church played a significant role in the preservation and transmission of the testimonies received.

The vigorous debates over the last several decades among the exegetes about the origin and growth of the gospel tradition and about its various settings help us all to see much more clearly how the New Testament was written and bring us closer to the unprecedented events of first-century Christianity. In the main, modern scholars recognize the unity of the cross and the resurrection and the importance of the resurrection for the salvation of mankind. With the help of this modern scholarship, this unity of the cross and the resurrection, which has always been present in the liturgical life of the Church, may now be seen in a new manner and in a new perspective.

There are other trends in modern scholarship, however, that point to a different and opposing view than the one we have just outlined. One of these trends is known to us as the "demythologization" of the gospel. For the demythologizers, the New Testament should be interpreted in existential terms. In studying the gospels as records of past events, they attempt to separate transcendent elements from human, natural ones, ascribing the former to the category of "myths." These scholars, therefore, treat the resurrection with skepticism, as an event outside normal human experience and understanding.

Among the most important of the modern scholars dealing

with the resurrection are the German Protestant theologians
Rudolf Bultmann and Willie Marxsen. For Rudolf Bultmann
the apostolic witness to the resurrection of Christ does not point
to an event that happened in history but is a reflection upon
or interpretation of the cross. "The Church had to surmount
the scandal of the cross and did it in the Easter faith," he
writes. Faith rooted in the resurrection is nothing but "faith
in the Word of preaching as the Word of God."[4] The death
of Christ without the word of preaching would be a tragic
event. According to Bultmann, whoever hears the word of
preaching and responds to it dies and rises with Christ. The
resurrection is an interpretation of the cross.

In discussing the crucifixion of Jesus, Bultmann makes a
distinction between the historical (*historisch*) and the historic
(*geschichtlich*) aspects of the event. The crucifixion itself
falls in the first category—it is an event that happened in history
and was watched by many. The resurrection, however, signifies
the redemptive aspect of the cross of Christ. The cross, then, is
historical, while the resurrection is a historic (*geschichtlich*)
interpretation of the event of the cross, whose significance was
conveyed through mythological language. Bultmann does not
distinguish between the event of the cross and the event of the
first Easter Sunday. The resurrection of Christ is not an event
by itself that followed the crucifixion; it is not an event of past
history but "the rise of faith in the risen Lord."[5] How faith in
the resurrection arose we do not know, he confesses, for the
rise of faith in the New Testament tradition has been obscured
by legends. The empty tomb and the appearances of Christ after
the resurrection are explicitly dismissed as nothing but legends,
created by the Church to embellish its tradition.[6] St Paul did
not know of any empty tomb, Bultmann asserts, and, referring
to the appearances listed by Paul in 1 Corinthians 15:5-8, he
concludes that the resurrection of Christ is really his exaltation
without resurrection in the ordinary sense of the term. Only

---

[4]Rudolf Bultmann, *Theology of the New Testament*, 2 vols. (New York:
Charles Scribner's Sons, 1951) 1:45.

[5]Idem, "New Testament and Mythology," in Hans Werner Bartsch, ed.,
Kerygma and Myth (New York: Harper Torchbooks, 1961) 42.

[6]Ibid., 39.

later was this exaltation interpreted as resurrection in the Church. Since the resurrection requires that the tomb was found empty, he continues, such an account was inserted in the New Testament narratives. All in all, to speak of the resurrection is not to speak of an event in history with a "self-evident meaning" but of a mythological event that takes place in the lives of men.[7]

Bultmann, commenting on the two terminologies found in the gospel accounts—that of resurrection and that of exaltation—presents the terminology of exaltation as the original.[8] He cannot accept the witness of the New Testament itself that the resurrection of Jesus is at the same time his exaltation and glorification. Christ was raised in glory with a glorified body. To speak of his resurrection is to understand his exaltation—they are inseparable. Here is the main difference between the resurrection of Christ and the resuscitation, the coming back to life, of Lazarus. Bultmann's insistence upon the exaltation as something separate and different from the resurrection allows him to dismiss the empty tomb and the appearances as non-historical and to characterize them as legends. However, it was the very terminology of resurrection, not that of exaltation, that became standard terminology in the New Testament, and the reason for this is that the terminology of exaltation was found less adequate for interpreting the facts and evidence of Christ's resurrection—particularly the fact of the discovery of the empty tomb.

After Bultmann's writings, Willie Marxsen's book *The Resurrection of Jesus of Nazareth* is probably the best-known discussion and examination of this subject by an exegete who offers a radical solution to the problem. Marxsen agrees with Bultmann that the resurrection is not a fact that stands by itself but a reflection of something else. But while for Bultmann the resurrection takes place in the lives of the disciples and all those who accept their testimony, for Marxsen it is a reflection

---

[7]For a succinct evaluation and criticism of Bultmann's demythologizing interpretation of salvation, see Gustaf Aulen, *The Drama and the Symbols: A Book on the Images of God and the Problems They Raise* (Philadelphia: Fortress Press, 1970) 174ff.

[8]On these two terminologies, see below, 35-7 and 81.

on the history of Jesus.[9] The main thing is not the resurrection of Christ but Jesus, as he was experienced in his earthly ministry.

Marxsen writes: "Now the fact that the raising from the dead occurred is not really fundamental, for to speak in such a way is after all *to turn into history what was the result of an interpretation.* This was no doubt *intelligible,* perhaps even necessary at that time, but it is *forbidden* to us in the present day."[10] He abandons the resurrection to emphasize the importance of the earthly Jesus. The resurrection to Marxsen is not an event that even requires a historical judgment. What actually happened cannot be proven from the viewpoint of contemporary faith, for faith does not inform us of what happened in the past. We could not know of the resurrection on the basis of our limited experience or on the basis of information we receive through the testimony of other people. They proclaim to us that Jesus is risen and ask us to believe in his resurrection, but if we ask them how it happened, "they give us their own ideas on the subject." Marxsen is quite explicit in stating that "it is quite impossible to deduce from the New Testament the reliability of the information about the mode of Jesus' resurrection." Why is this so? Because, he answers, for the New Testament authors the mode of the resurrection of Jesus was not of fundamental importance. He is risen, he is not dead but alive, "however one may care to think of this as taking place."

Marxsen is convinced that "the mode of resurrection" and any information about it do not belong to the integral part of our faith. We may associate the words "Jesus is risen" with more than one concept. Some will interpret these words as expressing the "bodily" resurrection of Jesus, while others may read in them a kind of "spiritual" resurrection, which may

[9]See Willie Marxsen, *The Resurrection of Jesus of Nazareth* (Philadelphia: Fortress Press, 1970) and his "Resurrection of Jesus as a Historical and Theological Problem," in C. F. D. Moule, ed., *The Significance of the Message of the Resurrection for Faith in Jesus Christ,* Studies in Biblical Theology, 2d series, 8 (London: SCM Press, 1968) 15-50. See also in the same volume Hans-Georg Geyer, "The Resurrection of Jesus Christ: A Survey of the Debate in Present Day Theology," 105-35.

[10]Marxsen, "The Resurrection of Jesus as a Historical and Theological Problem," 48.

not differ from the Hellenistic concept of the disembodied soul. Either interpretation would be possible, because for Marxsen the words "Jesus is risen" mean "I believe, I am involved." He continues with this existential interpretation and concludes that "the mode of resurrection," whatever it may be—the resurrection from the tomb or the immortality of the soul—is not an essential part of our present involvement. To him "the content of the preaching of the resurrection does not have to include the way in which the crucified Jesus rose." Jesus lives "in faith kindled through preaching. But faith cannot tell how he became alive." In the way this theory is constructed it is not surprising that Marxsen easily dismisses the evidence of the empty tomb, for his view of the resurrection does not require it. Furthermore, he reduces all the resurrection appearances to one, the appearance to Peter, which in his view is the only one that is "constitutive" for faith.[11] There is no doubt that Marxsen came to this position by a radical reduction of the New Testament witness.[12] His exegesis supports his predetermined position.

Both Bultmann and Marxsen use the historical method of interrogating the text, which in principle excludes all that cannot be reduced to the level of human existence. Nobody has described this method better than Bultmann himself: "The historical method includes the presupposition that history is a unity in the sense of a closed continuum of effects in which individual events are connected by the succession of cause and effect . . . This closeness means that the continuum of historical happenings cannot be rent by interference of supernatural, transcendent powers and that therefore there is no 'miracle' in this sense of the word."[13] Rejection of God's intervention in history appears to be built into such a method itself.

[11]See, in particular, the chapter on "The Miracle of the Resurrection" in Marxsen's book *The Resurrection of Jesus of Nazareth,* 112-29.

[12]Raymond E. Brown writes that he "would reject as hypercriticism Marxsen's attempt to reduce the Pauline list *ad absurdum* by dwelling on the problem of . . . possible duplications, as well as his argument that only the appearance to Peter was constitutive for faith." See his *The Virginal Conception and Bodily Resurrection of Jesus* (New York: Paulist Press, 1973) 96, n164.

[13]See Bultmann's essay "Is Exegesis without Presuppositions?" in *Exis-*

Demythologization of the Resurrection

For Bultmann and his followers, the resurrection is a "faith event." Jesus, according to them, rose in the faith of his disciples, not in history. They deny that the resurrection took place in history. This is a logical and expected result of the application of Bultmann's method to the New Testament gospels, and yet there is a paradox in his interpretation of this "faith event." On the one hand, Bultmann tried to demonstrate that we know very little, almost nothing, of the historical Jesus, due to the many legends created by the Church. But on the other hand, he implied by his theory of the "faith event" that this Jesus of Nazareth exercised great power and authority, and that he made a very unusual impact upon his followers. And this impact must have had a historical basis.

In attempting to make the gospel message acceptable to modern man, Bultmann and Marxsen have removed the very basis of the New Testament faith. The faith they try to save is no longer rooted in anything concrete and is not sustained by a living presence of the transcendent Reality. It is hard to see how modern men and women can come to faith without the knowledge and experience of the reality that transcends their existence and gives meaning to it.

The order of the gospels—the empty tomb, the appearances that gave evidence for faith and the spiritual experience of the resurrection in daily life—is not the order of the modern demythologizers of the resurrection. Their way of thinking, however, is not so modern. Their mistrust of the records of the

tence and Faith (New York: Meridian Books, 1960) 291-2. Gustave Martelet has pointed out that Bultmann's historical method forbids history itself to present "evidence of any action which cannot be reduced to the purely human order." Continuing with a succinct analysis of the exclusion of miracles by this method, he comments on how this method conceives of faith as being produced by the mind, for "it cannot depend upon a transcendent event made plain in history." In conclusion he pointedly adds: "If we reject in principle the historical possibility of a more than human action . . . then we are basing our hermeneutics not on the *meaning* of the texts but on the *ideas* in the reader's mind." See Martelet's *The Risen Christ and the Eucharistic World* (New York: Seabury Press, 1976) 63-4.

gospels is something that they hold in common with the early docetics and gnostics. Although separated by centuries, neither can believe that Jesus lived in the manner the gospels describe or that he taught as our primary sources indicate. Skeptical of the truthfulness of the gospels, both the ancient gnostics and the modern demythologizers find themselves engaged in producing their own myth and their own Christ. To demythologize an event that belongs to the life of Jesus is to remove it from history, and in the process the gospel is emptied of its content and historical character. Christ then ceases to be the "good news" himself—he becomes only the revealer of the good news. H.A. Williams, in his engaging book *True Resurrection,* contends that such modern attempts to explain the facts of revelation aim "to soften their impact upon us" or to "reduce the sheer brutality of the fact" to something more digestible and thus acceptable.[14] Pinchas Lapide, a Jewish New Testament scholar who recently published *Resurrection—A Jewish Faith Experience,* commented in one of his public appearances in Germany that the demythologizers of Easter are "sawing off the branch of faith upon which they are sitting" when they assign the resurrection to the subjective realm of faith.[15]

The demythologizers distort the meaning of the resurrection and minimize the importance of the event for apologetic and pastoral reasons, to make it seem more acceptable to modern man. They make their sources attest to what they feel modern man would like to hear and believe. But in their attempt to make the faith alive and relevant they have achieved results quite opposite to what they were aiming at. Their ideas are stimulating, but their judgment of what is authentic and what is not, what is fact and what is legend, are at best subjective and questionable.

[14]H. A. Williams, *True Resurrection* (New York: Harper & Row, 1972) 136. Williams defines the resurrection of Christ as an "experienced miracle" which is neither explanation nor theory. He then adds that it "may be that Christianity as an explanatory system, as a theodicy, will soon collapse because as an explanatory system it always contained within itself the seeds of its own corruption." Yet we shall not lose any of the truth and power of the resurrection, for "the heralded collapse may be precisely the death which is always the necessary prelude to resurrection" (142).

[15]Reported in *Time* (May 7, 1979).

Marxsen and Bultmann, however, have influenced even important representatives of the Catholic tradition, who use their terminology even if they do not quite accept or share their arguments or conclusions. This has been pointed out by Reginald H. Fuller, in his review of Edward Schillebeeckx's *Jesus: An Experiment in Christology.* In his discussion of the resurrection, Schillebeeckx identifies the empty tomb narrative in Mark, Matthew and Luke as "a local Jerusalem cult narrative which *presupposes the resurrection faith."* But is there behind this account an actual report of the women who in the gospels discovered the empty tomb? Fuller, the author of *The Formation of the Resurrection Narratives,*[16] concludes that "Schillebeeckx leaves in doubt whether the tomb story has any factual origin." He also sees in Schillebeeckx's treatment of the post-resurrection appearances language that is "strongly reminiscent" of Bultmann—"who said that the Easter event is the coming of the disciples to faith in the redemptive significance of the cross"—and Marxsen—"who says that Easter means that 'the cause of Jesus continues.' "[17]

The gospel records indicate that the resurrection is an external event that reveals a transcendent reality and therefore cannot be reduced to a subjective vision. History and faith here are not independent but include each other. The first witnesses to the resurrection saw clearly the difference between the risen Christ and Christ as he was during his public ministry, yet they were never tempted to separate the "historical Jesus" from the "Christ of faith." When he appeared to them they recognized him as one and the same person.[18] Faith in the risen Christ was born during these post-resurrection meetings and cannot be separated from the actual event of the resur-

[16]Reginald H. Fuller, *The Formation of the Resurrection Narratives* (New York: Macmillan, 1971).

[17]Later, in a discussion of the term "Easter experience," Schillebeeckx takes a stance quite different from Marxsen, to the surprise of the reviewer. But Fuller persists in questioning and attempting to clarify Schillebeeckx's position and finally asks: "Is Schillebeeckx prepared to go beyond Marxsen and say that the Easter event is primarily not what God did to the disciples but what God did to Jesus?" See Fuller's review in *Interpretation* 34:3 (1980) 295-6.

[18]He was present and was breaking bread with them both before and after his death and resurrection. After his resurrection, however, "his presence is strange; his coming shocks," and "he no longer comes and goes, but 'appears'

rection. The event to which they bear witness remains both the source and the object of their faith. The terms they use to proclaim the resurrection indicate what happened and at the same time reveal their absolute conviction that Jesus was resurrected bodily. "Jesus is risen" means not that he is risen into the proclamation of the Church, nor are these words merely reflections on his public ministry—they mean that he is risen from the tomb, from the "pangs of death."

According to the New Testament and the tradition of the Church, by raising Jesus from the dead God affected all mankind and revealed what would happen to the entire creation. The fathers of the early Church constantly affirmed that what has already happened to Christ in his resurrection will happen to us as well. Along with St Paul, they hoped for the transformation of all creation. "I think that what we suffer in this life can never be compared to the glory, as yet unrevealed, which is waiting for us. The whole creation is eagerly waiting for God to reveal his sons" (Rm 8:18-19 JB). As St John Chrysostom stresses, when Christ enters into his glory it is the work of the Father for the sake of all men and not for the sake of one only. Christ's resurrection is the beginning of the resurrection of all men—it is a new creation. This is what the Church has proclaimed throughout the centuries in the Nicene Creed: "I look for the resurrection of the dead, and the life of the world to come."

---

and 'vanishes' with disturbing suddenness," writes Romano Guardini in *The Lord* (New York: Meridian Books, 1969) 410. Actually, this is a description of the difference that the resurrection made. See below, 32, 96, 152 (n53).

2

Resurrection and "Resurrections"

The idea of resurrection was known to the religions of the Near East before the rise of the Christian movement. The Christian hope of the resurrection of the dead had its origin in the Jewish hope of the resurrection at the end of time. Yet only in Christianity is the resurrection the predominant and controlling factor in faith and worship.

The Christian Church began with the message of the resurrection of Christ, not with an idea of deliverance or an expression of faith in future salvation. The difference between Christianity, on the one hand, and all other religions, including Judaism, on the other, is asserted in the apostolic proclamation that the resurrection of Jesus of Nazareth had already taken place in history—an idea inconceivable in the Jewish tradition. The Christians insisted that the glory of future resurrection had already been revealed in the past. The nature of Jewish expectations of the Messiah and the resurrection at the end of time was radically changed, for salvation for Christians now depended on being incorporated into the body of the Messiah who died and rose from the dead.

There is a widely held view that Christianity was influenced by many cults and mystery religions in the Roman world. The school of the history of religions, which flourished in Germany in the early twentieth century, and its successors have been particularly adamant in maintaining this position. They insist that the theology of Paul and his doctrine of redemption by the death and resurrection of Christ were especially affected by the Hellenistic cults. Yet upon further examination we shall see that nothing in these cults and mysteries corresponds to the essential faith and message of the primitive Church.

Resurrection in the Old Testament and in Judaism at the Time of Christ

The ancient Hebrews believed that when a man dies he goes down to Sheol, a place of gloom where existence cannot be identified with the word life but rather is something like "sleep or rest, a torpor occasionally penetrated by a few flashes of consciousness, inactivity, levelling out all inequalities between individuals."[1] According to the New Testament witness, Jesus descended into Hades (the Greek word for the Hebrew Sheol) but was "not abandoned to Hades," his body "did not experience corruption," but God raised him to life (Acts 2:31-32). It was impossible for him to be held in the power of Hades or Sheol (Acts 2:24).

In the biblical tradition there are two views about liberation from Sheol: continuation in the collective life of the people of Israel and individual deliverance. The people of God whose life and history are recorded in the scriptures regarded life on earth as persisting in the family, tribe or nation of Israel. This concept of corporate personality or corporate survival was maintained throughout their history and was never completely replaced by the later teaching of individual deliverance. Concern for the future of the community usually accompanied interest in the individual within the community.

Jewish apocalyptic literature, along with the apocalyptic sections of the prophetic books, seems to promise individual liberation from death as well. We already find such an indication in the section of the book of the prophet Isaiah known as the "Apocalypse of Isaiah" (Is 24-27): "Thy dead shall live, their bodies shall rise. O dwellers in the dust, awake and sing for joy! For thy dew is a dew of light, and on the land of the shades thou wilt let it fall" (26:19). Here the prophet goes

---

[1]André-Marie Dubarle, "Belief in Immortality in the Old Testament and Judaism," in Pierre Benoit and Roland Murphy, eds., *Immortality and Resurrection* (New York: Herder and Herder, 1970) 37-8.

beyond the hope of the survival of the nation, of the people as a whole, and speaks of the resurrection of individuals within the context of national restoration. The same hope is spelled out more explicitly in the book of Daniel: "And many of those who sleep in the dust of the earth shall awake, some to everlasting life, and some to shame and everlasting contempt" (12:2). The language of resurrection from the dead is used here in the context of judgment and restoration. The author, a Jew who lived during the persecutions of Antiochus Epiphanes (167-164 B.C.), expressed a firm hope that pious Jews who suffered martyrdom would triumph by the power of God. Their piety was the cause of their deaths, but it would be rewarded in the future.[2]

The language of resurrection found in Daniel was used both in preexilic as well as exilic prophetic literature, but not as a promise of individual resurrection.[3] Both Ezekiel in chapter 37 and Hosea in 5:15-6:3 speak of national renewal and the people's return to the Lord in these terms, but only later were these passages interpreted as a promise of general resurrection. The prophet Ezekiel uses the rising of the people from their graves as an image of national restoration: "Thus says the Lord God: Behold, I will open your graves, and raise you from your graves, O my people; and I will bring you home into the land of Israel" (37:12). Here Ezekiel is speaking about the return of the people of Israel from Babylonian exile, emphasizing that there will be no renewal without the initiative of God and his power. Hosea, a preexilic prophet, describes the return of the people to the Lord after national apostasy and betrayal: "Come, let us return to the Lord; for he has torn, that he may heal us; he has stricken, and he will bind us up. After two days he will revive us; on the third day he will raise us up, that we may live before him" (6:1-2). These words were also later interpreted by some rabbis as a promise of general resurrection.[4]

---

[2]See George W. E. Nickelsburg, *Resurrection, Immortality, and Eternal Life in Intertestamental Judaism* (Cambridge, Mass.: Harvard University Press, 1972) 17ff.

[3]Ibid.

[4]Among Christians, Tertullian was the first to use this verse in connection

At the time that the apostle Paul was elaborating his theology of the resurrection, two basic views concerning individual resurrection were current in Judaism. One conceived of the resurrection in a crude, physical manner, as a return to the life already lived and known—those who had physical defects before death would also have them in the life after the resurrection. The other view was expressive of a more spiritualized concept of resurrection.

The first view was undoubtedly the more popular. It is predominant in the second book of Maccabees (7 and 14), which was composed during the first century B.C. In 2 Maccabees 7 we have the story of the martyrdom of seven brothers and their mother who were put to death during the persecutions under Antiochus Epiphanes because they remained faithful to the law and refused to obey the pagan king's command to eat unclean foods. In their suffering the seven brothers and their mother supported and encouraged one another, and they all died nobly with the hope of resurrection. When the second brother was at his last breath he said to the king: "You dismiss us from this present life, but the king of the universe will raise us up to an everlasting renewal of life, because we have died for his laws" (7:9). The third brother expressed the hope that whatever the enemy would cut off from his body he would get back again (7:11). Finally, when the youngest son was taken to be tortured, the mother addressed him with this last advice:

> I beseech you, my child, to look at the heaven and the earth and see everything that is in them and recognize that God did not make them out of things that existed. Thus also mankind comes into being. Do not fear this butcher, but prove worthy of your brothers. Accept death, so that in God's mercy I may get you back again with your brothers. (7:27-29)

The hope of resurrection is linked here with the power of God, which he displayed in the creation of the world and

with Christ's resurrection. See Joachim Jeremias, *New Testament Theology: The Proclamation of Jesus* (New York: Charles Scribner's Sons, 1971) 304.

of mankind. Those who are created by God and killed by his enemies because of their obedience to him and his law will one day be vindicated—God will return to his martyrs what the king has taken away by torture. A similar idea is expressed in 14:37-46, in the story of the martyrdom of a certain Razis, one of the elders of Jerusalem, who expected his body to be restored in the resurrection. At the end of this account Razis tears out his entrails, takes them in his hands and hurls them at the crowd, "calling upon the Lord of life and spirit to give them back to him again" (14:46).

This view of resurrection as a return or reawakening was also presented in 2 Baruch 49 and 50. Written in the last quarter of the first century A.D. by several orthodox Jews, this book is also known as the Syrian Apocalypse of Baruch because it is preserved in a Syriac version. The passage most important for our purposes is 49:1-50:2, dealing with the nature of the resurrected body. Baruch asks the Mighty One: "In what shape will those live who live in Thy day? Or how will the splendour of those who [are] after that time continue? Will they then resume this form of the present, and put on these entrammelling members, which are now involved in evils, and in which evils are consummated, or wilt Thou perchance change these things which have been in the world as also the world?" (49:1-3) The Mighty One answered him:

> Hear, Baruch, this word, and write in the remembrance of thy heart all that thou shalt learn. For the earth shall then assuredly restore the dead, which it now receives, in order to preserve them. It shall make no change in their form, but as it has received, so shall it restore them, and as I delivered them unto it, so also shall it raise them. (50:1-2)[5]

The Sadducees, who did not believe in the resurrection, reflected this attitude in the account of the hypothetical question they asked Jesus (Mt 22:23-28). There were seven

---

[5] All quotes from the apocryphal (noncanonical) Old Testament books are taken from R. H. Charles, *The Apocrypha and Pseudepigrapha of the Old Testament,* 2 vols. (Oxford: Clarendon Press, 1913).

brothers. The first married and died childless, and the Sadducees asked what would happen if the rest of the brothers, one
after the other, following the law of Moses, all married the
widow and died childless, and finally the woman herself died.
"In the resurrection, therefore, to which of the seven will she
be wife?" (22:28) Jesus indicated in his answer their ignorance of the scriptures and of the power of God.

The two passages in the gospels where the risen Christ
showed his disciples his hands and feet (Lk 24:39) or his
hands and side (Jn 20:27) do not necessarily reflect the influence of this popular view of resurrection. These two accounts
of the post-resurrection appearances are meant to express and
underline the identity of the risen Christ with the crucified Jesus
of Nazareth: "See my hands and my feet, that it is I myself
[ὅτι ἐγώ εἰμι αὐτός]." The same body that was crucified
was resurrected. And yet something had happened to that body
—it was transformed and glorified. Thomas, invited to touch
his hands and his side, could only reply without touching them
"My Lord and my God!" (Jn 20:28) Christ's resurrection is
not simply a return to his previously known earthly existence,
as was the case with Lazarus (Jn 11), the daughter of Jairus
(Mk 5) and the son of the widow of Nain (Lk 7). They were
not changed, they would die again and wait for the resurrection of the last days. Their resurrections, however, anticipate
the final resurrection, after which there will be no more death.
The resurrection of Christ is the reality of this future which
has already occurred. Christ was raised from the dead, from
the mortal condition—unlike Lazarus, who was simply brought
back to life. Thus, the resurrection of Christ is the end of the
old and the beginning of the new creation.

A more spiritual concept of resurrection was also known
to the teachers of Judaism. In 2 Baruch, besides the popular
physical view of resurrection, we find in chapter 51 another
view that contains an element of exaltation or spiritual transformation:

> And it shall come to pass, when that appointed day has
> gone by, that then shall the aspect of those who are
> condemned be afterwards changed, and the glory of

those who now act wickedly shall become worse than it is, as they shall suffer torment. Also for the glory of those who have now been justified in My law, who have had understanding in their life, and who have planted in their heart the root of wisdom, then their splendour shall be glorified in changes, and the form of their face shall be turned into the light of their beauty, that they may be able to acquire and receive the world which does not die, which is then promised to them. (51:1-3)

One of the most important intertestamental books for our understanding of resurrection in Judaism is 1 Enoch.[6] Here we find the assertion that "The righteous and elect shall have risen from the earth, and ceased to be of downcast countenance. And they shall have been clothed with garments of glory, and these shall be the garments of life from the Lord of Spirits; and your garments shall not grow old, nor your glory pass away before the Lord of Spirits" (62:15-16; cf 108:11ff). There is a significant difference between 2 Baruch 51 and 1 Enoch in their approach to the future resurrection. The author or authors of 2 Baruch conceived of the transformation of the body as taking place after the resurrection, not together with it. In 1 Enoch, on the other hand, the resurrection does not always include the body (see 102-104). The spirits of the sinners will descend into Sheol to face judgment and torment. At the moment of death the spirits of the righteous will also descend into Sheol, but at the judgment they will leave Sheol and ascend to heaven.[7]

We can also find a spiritual concept of resurrection in 2 Esdras. Yet we must approach and evaluate references to resurrection in this book with caution. It is an apocalypse, the main part of which (chapters 3-14) was written at the end of the first century A.D. and whose author was presumably a Palestinian Jew. The first part of the book, however, which contains the references to a more spiritual view of resurrec-

[6]In the view of R. H. Charles, 1 Enoch is "for history of theological development the most important pseudepigrapha of the first two centuries B.C." See ibid., 2:163.

[7]Nickelsburg, 123f.

tion, was added in the middle of the second century by an unknown Christian, according to modern critics. Thus, the references to the resurrection are most likely heavily influenced by
the New Testament.[8]

Leaving aside this Christian interpolation into 2 Esdras,
what we find in the Jewish apocalyptic literature is quite sufficient to support the view that some spiritually minded Jews
would have found St Paul's references to a "transformed body"
congenial to them,[9] but they could not have anticipated that the
body would be glorified in history. They anticipated a future
resurrection either of the body or of the soul. The author of 1
Enoch, for instance, speaks of a future resurrection of the
spirits of the righteous. Others believed in a resurrection of the
untransfigured body, and still others looked forward to the
transformation of the body. They all moved beyond the Old
Testament view of a shadowy existence in Sheol, which cannot
be described as "life," and expected much more after death
than the teaching about Sheol would allow.[10]

Physical death was not considered by all of them to be an
important factor in their concept of resurrection. According
to the Wisdom of Solomon, which was written probably by a
Hellenistic Jew in the first century B.C., the souls of the righteous do not really die—they are in the hand of God, and only
"in the eyes of the foolish they seemed to have died" (3:1-2).
The death of the righteous is conceived of as their ascent to

---

[8]The first important reference to the resurrection in 2 Esdras occurs when
Ezra addresses the nations: "Rise and stand, and see at the feast of the Lord
the number of those who have been sealed. Those who have departed from
the shadow of this age have received glorious garments from the Lord" (2:39).
This is not yet the final resurrection, however. Their garments symbolize their
proximity to the throne of God, but they still await the day of judgment (cf
Rv 6:9ff). The second reference is given in the context of Ezra's vision of a
great multitude, in whose midst Ezra saw a young man, "and on the head
of each of them he placed a crown, but he was more exalted than they." When
Ezra asks who these people are and who the young man is, an angel replies:
"These are they who have put off mortal clothing and have put on the immortal, and they have confessed the name of God" and "He is the Son of
God, whom they confessed in the world" (2:42-47). The Christian influence
is clearly seen here.

[9]See W. D. Davies, *Paul and Rabbinic Judaism* (New York: Harper
Torchbooks, 1965) 308.

[10]Nickelsburg, 178f.

the presence of God, who "tested them and found them worthy of himself; like gold in the furnace he tried them, and like a sacrificial burnt offering he accepted them" (3:5-6). The unrighteous, the ungodly, go to their punishment.

There is a variety of views among the ancient rabbis with regard to the final destiny of human beings. Their teachings on this subject cannot be reduced to one unified, common teaching. Nevertheless, all their views differed significantly from what the apostles saw and experienced after the resurrection of Jesus. As Joachim Jeremias writes: "Nowhere in Jewish literature do we find a resurrection to δόξα [glory] as an event of history. Rather resurrection to δόξα—always and without exception means the dawn of God's creation. Therefore the disciples must have experienced the appearances of the Risen Lord as an eschatological event, as a dawning of a turning point of the world."[11]

Terminologies of Resurrection

The Old Testament and Jewish literature offered the followers of the risen Christ more than one set of expressions for describing and interpreting his resurrection. The first terminological source they might have used was in the Old Testament stories of Enoch and Elijah. Enoch "walked with God" and "God took him" (Gn 5:24). Elijah ascended to heaven in a chariot of fire (2 Kg 2:1-12). Both are mentioned in the New Testament—Enoch is listed in the genealogy of Jesus (Lk 3:37) and the prophet Elijah appeared and spoke with Christ on the mountain during his transfiguration (Mk 9:2-8; Mt 17:1-8; Lk 9:28-36). Yet while we would have expected the disciples of Christ, who were rooted in the scriptures, to use the terms and images already known to them from the stories of Enoch and Elijah, they preferred to use the term "resurrection" for a compelling reason. Jesus died and was raised from the dead, whereas neither Enoch nor Elijah passed through death. The death of Christ and his bodily resurrection exclude any similarity to the transfer of Enoch and Elijah to heaven.

[11]Jeremias, 308-9.

Jesus was raised from the dead and ascended to the Father.
The terms "taken up" or "ascent" by themselves do not necessarily imply resurrection. The New Testament authors use both
a terminology of resurrection and a terminology of exaltation
or glorification to present the victory of Christ over death and
his entrance into a new level of existence. The terminology of
exaltation would have been too vague if it were not linked with
that of resurrection. Exaltation by itself does not imply resurrection, but resurrection does imply exaltation in the New
Testament.[12] The terms and images used for the final destiny
of Enoch and Elijah were therefore inadequate to describe the
resurrection of Christ. Moreover, what happened to Christ on
the day of his resurrection and ascension affected all men, for
"in fact Christ has been raised from the dead, the first fruits
of those who have fallen asleep" (1 Cor 15:20).

There was still one more set of terms available already to
the New Testament Christians for possible use in interpreting
the resurrection of Christ. This was the dualistic terminology
used in the Wisdom of Solomon (3:1-4). The Essenes, who
withdrew into the wilderness to preserve the purity of the law,
shared the teaching of the book of Wisdom. They too did
not look upon physical death as an important factor in their
speculation about the destiny of man. Like the author of the
Wisdom of Solomon, the Essenes minimized the significance of
physical death.[13] In their view, souls were not perishable, and
only souls reached the realm of bliss.[14] Where death is not
taken seriously it is of no consequence what happens to the
body. Neither the transformation nor the glorification of the

---

[12]G. O'Collins, *The Easter Jesus* (London: Darton, Longman and Todd,
1973) 50ff.

[13]Nickelsburg, 166f.

The Essenes held that "bodies are corruptible, and the matter they are made
of are not permanent; but that the souls are immortal, and continue forever,
and that they come out of the most subtle air, and are united to their bodies
as to prisons, into which they are drawn by a certain natural enticement; but
that when they are set free from the bonds of the flesh, they then, as released
from a long bondage, rejoice and mount upward." Flavius Josephus, *The Great
Roman-Jewish War* (New York: Harper Torchbooks, 1960) 2:8:11.

[14]T. H. Gaster, "Resurrection," in G. A. Buttrick, ed., *The Interpreter's
Dictionary of the Bible*, 4 vols. (New York: Abingdon Press, 1962) 4:42.

body play any obvious role in the Wisdom of Solomon or among those who share its theology.

The gospel writers make no concession to a dualistic interpretation of body and soul. A dualistic perspective would not have admitted real resurrection, that is, the resurrection of the whole human being. Therefore, the New Testament deliberately excludes this dualistic terminology from its interpretation of the event of the resurrection. What happened to Christ and what he revealed about himself to his disciples during his appearances forced the disciples to give new meaning to the existing vocabulary of resurrection. For the contemporaries of Christ, the term "resurrection" carried with it the faith that God would manifest his power and would bring human beings back to life, and this would be a sign that the messianic age had arrived. The message of Easter is that the end is already here, the Messiah has come. The new humanity has been inaugurated with his coming and his resurrection.

The language of the resurrection is clear, and there is no doubt as to what the New Testament witnesses wished to express. The terminology itself, however, has never been a reason for rejecting the resurrection of Christ. What has been difficult to accept, both for ancient as well as modern man, is what this language points to as an event in history. If we reject one particular miracle recorded in the gospels, the resurrection of Lazarus or the resurrection of Christ, we do so not because the language in these accounts is ambiguous or misleading. We understand the language, but we reject the event for the simple reason that we are skeptical that it occurred as it is told.[15] The terminology of resurrection *and* glorification used in the New Testament is best suited to express the evidence of the bodily transformation of Christ as well as to indicate what actually happened in history, for this terminology takes into account both the empty tomb and the appearances of the risen Christ. We must therefore conclude that there is no other resurrection account in the Bible that would correspond to the story of the

[15]See Gustave Martelet, *The Risen Christ and the Eucharistic World* (New York: Seabury Press, 1976) 62-4.

resurrection of Jesus. God raised his Son from the dead and
made him "both Lord and Christ" (Acts 2:32, 36).

Resurrection and the Mystery Cults

Some interpreters have tried to explain the resurrection on
the basis of the mystery cults. This question of the relationship
between Christianity and the mystery religions has interested
believers as well as nonbelievers, obviously for different reasons. The parallels are indeed striking: the death of the mythic
deity, his descent into the underworld, his disappearance for
a short time, his reappearance and ascent. All this provides a
framework that can be detected in the New Testament itself.

The fathers of the Church were well acquainted with this
outward similarity of framework, and regarded it as a sign
that God was active in the gentile world, preparing it for the
future coming of Christ, in whom all of their deep-seated yearning for salvation would be fulfilled. This attitude toward the
pagan world and its religions was influenced by St Paul's views
and insights in Acts 14 and 17, as well as in his Epistle to the
Romans. God "created every race of men of one stock, to in-
habit the whole earth's surface. He fixed the epochs of their
history and the limits of their territory. They were to seek God,
and, it might be, touch and find him; though indeed he is not
far from each one of us, for in him we live and move, in him
we exist" (Acts 17:26-28 NEB). God never abandoned the
pagan world; he spoke to all mankind through his creation,
through the requirements of the law which are written on their
hearts. Their consciences bear witness to him (Rm 2:14f).
God did not deprive himself of witnesses in the pagan world
(Acts 14:16f). Pagan religions are the responses of pagan
man to this fragmentary, incomplete revelation. Some of the
early Christian fathers even proposed a theory of "borrowing"
to explain certain truths contained in these pagan religions.
St Justin the Martyr, in his *First Apology* (54-55), goes so far
as to claim that the ancient philosophers and pagan religions
"borrowed" from Moses, in whose writings the gospel was

prophesied, although he stresses that the crucifixion was never imitated by "any of the so-called sons of Zeus."

When the fathers evaluated the pagan religions, they usually spoke in terms of God's condescension (συγκατάβασις). Everything in God's relations with man is seen as condescension. For the salvation of his lost sheep, God allowed himself to be honored with the rites that the pagans used. By condescending, he leads them to the full light. His love is the source of his condescension, and the principal result and climax of it is the incarnation of his Son.[16]

The mystery religions were men's protest against the meaninglessness of events, as M. Nilsson has observed.[17] They were a protest against astrology, which assumed that the rays of the seven planets of ancient astronomy determine the lives and fortunes of those born under them. The entire destiny not only of individuals but also of states was thought to depend on the stars—the moment of birth determines the moment of death. Against this strict causality the voice of the mystery religions was raised, offering salvation from destiny and from astrology. A mystery was a secret rite in which the individual participated of his own free choice and by which he was put into a closer relationship with a particular deity. Those being initiated into a mystery received an experience, were put into a certain frame of mind. Aristotle interpreted participation in the mysteries as an emotional experience through which a person passed without learning a sacred doctrine. The mystery religions satisfied the thirst for religious emotions and gave the initiates the illusion of absolute certainty of being saved from fate.

Among the most important mystery religions was that of

---

[16]Henri Pinard de la Boullaye wrote a celebrated essay on the thesis of condescension from the point of view of the history of religions, in which he deals with St Justin, Tertullian, Clement of Alexandria, Origen, St Athanasius, St Cyril of Alexandria, St John Chrysostom, St Gregory Nazianzen and St Augustine—"Les infiltrations païennes dans l'Ancienne Loi d'après les Pères de l'Église: La Thèse de la Condescendance," *Recherches de Science Religieuse* 9 (1919) 197-221. See also Jean Danielou, *God and the Ways of Knowing* (New York: Meridian Books, 1957) 16ff.

[17]See Martin P. Nilsson's important study *Greek Piety* (Oxford: Clarendon Press, 1948).

the Great Mother of the gods and the youth Attis. On a speci-
fied night, when Attis would be laid upon a portable bier and
mourned, the priest would anoint the throats of all present
and whisper to them: "Take courage, ye mystae, the god is
saved, so shall salvation be ours."[18] There were also the Syrian
Baals and the Greek Adonis, the Egyptian Queen Isis and the
Lord Serapis. All these were the focus of primitive rites based
on the cycle of nature which, under the influence of Hellenism,
were interpreted, elaborated and transformed into mystery
religions of personal salvation.[19]

What separates Christianity from the mystery religions is
obviously the person of Christ. The mysteries did not present
a man who lived a human life, died and rose again. Deities
such as Adonis, Attis and Osiris were not sent like Christ, they
never "became flesh and dwelt among us" (Jn 1:14), they
never experienced human emotions, hunger and fatigue—as
Jesus did—and they were never really dead and buried in a
tomb. They were vegetation deities who in late antiquity came
to be regarded as human beings of the mythical primal period.[20]
There is a world of difference between the incarnate Son of
God, who was recognized as a living, historical man by his
disciples as well as by his opponents, and these gods of the
mysteries.[21]

A number of scholars have also raised the question of paral-
lelism between Christianity and the gnostic idea of the Son
of God, the heavenly redeemer become man. But did the gnostics really teach about a Son of God who was sent into the
world and who assumed human nature before the Christians
themselves did? Several leading researchers in the field of the
New Testament and gnosticism have pointed out the lack of
any incontestable evidence of a gnostic redeemer myth before

[18]Frederick C. Grant, ed., *Hellenistic Religions* (New York: Liberal Arts
Press, 1953) 146.

[19]On the cults, see Nilsson, 150f.

[20]For an excellent discussion on this point see Martin Hengel, *The Son of
God: The Origin of Christology and the History of Jewish-Hellenistic Religion*
(Philadelphia: Fortress Press, 1976) 21-30.

[21]Geoffrey Parrinder, *Avatar and Incarnation: The Wilde Lectures in Natural and Comparative Religion in the University of Oxford* (New York:
Barnes and Noble, 1970) 210.

the rise of Christianity. Martin Hengel states flatly that "there is no gnostic redeemer myth in the sources which can be demonstrated chronologically to be pre-Christian,"[22] while Arthur D. Nock emphasizes that "early Christianity itself was a catalyst in the rise of gnostic systems" and that faith in the incarnate Christ "precipitated elements previously suspended in solution."[23] It is no longer profitable for us to pose the question of how much gnosticism influenced Christianity. The question now is of Christian influence on the development of the gnostic movement and of how much and in what way gnosticism borrowed from Christianity in producing its redeemer myth.[24]

One respected authority and reliable guide to the life and practices of Roman paganism, F. Cumont, has observed how Christian ideas influenced the enemies of Christianity, the members of the mystery cults as well as the gnostics.[25] Students of the mystery cults in general suggest that Christian influence, together with an interest in interpreting the myths allegorically, led to a spiritualization of their content and practices. Thus, the final cause of similarity between Christianity and the cults, in the words of Hugo Rahner, is found in "the growing influence of Christianity to which in late antiquity the cults themselves began to be subject, a development to which recent scholarship has become increasingly alive."[26]

---

[22]Hengel, 33.

[23]*Essays on Religion and the Ancient World,* 2:958, quoted in Hengel, 34.

[24]See Robert M. Grant, *An Historical Introduction to the New Testament* (New York: Harper & Row, 1963) 203.

[25]F. Cumont, *The Oriental Religions in Roman Paganism* (Chicago: Open Court, 1911) xviii.

There was a particular rite, for example, called *taurobolium,* or baptism in blood, in which the blood of a slain bull was considered to have redeeming power—an analogy to Christian baptism. In this rite a bull was slain over a covered pit, and the person being baptized received the blood all over his body. According to inscriptions that have been found, the effect of the *taurobolium* (literally "shooting of the bull") was supposed to last about twenty years. Later inscriptions, however, written under Christian influence after the pagans started using Christian terminology, suggest that the rite provides eternal escape from death.

[26]This is particularly true for the period of the fourth century, when the Christian Church and liturgical practices became dominant. See Hugo Rahner, *Greek Myth and Christian Mystery* (New York: Harper & Row, 1963) 42f.

The Different Origins of the Church and the Mystery Cults

The use of certain basic terms in the early Christian Church and in the mystery religions adds support to our view that they sprang from different sources. To give just two examples, let us examine how the terms ἐγείρειν (to raise up, to rise) and μυστήριον (mystery, secret) are used in the New Testament and in the records of the mystery religions.

The verb ἐγείρειν is one of the key words found in the resurrection passages of the gospels and the epistles, and it is also found in two important prophecies concerning the resurrection in the Greek translation of the Old Testament (Is 26:19 and Dn 12:2). In secular Greek, however, it seldom appears in reference to resurrection. The noun ἔγερσις (rise, rising), on the other hand, although fairly common in Hellenistic Greek, is avoided by the New Testament authors, who used it only once, in Matthew 27:53.[27] Otherwise, the writers of the New Testament preferred the verb, as if to emphasize the reality and uniqueness of Christ's resurrection. By contrast, the verb ἐγείρειν is scarcely used at all in reference to the rising of the savior gods in the mystery cults. Their records tell us rather that "the god is delivered" or that "he lives," not that he is raised up.[28]

The second term, μυστήριον, is well attested to both in the New Testament and in the mystery cults, but in different contexts and with profoundly different meanings. Our main source for the meaning of the Christian "mystery" in the New Testament is St Paul, who uses the term more than twenty times in his epistles. Here are three representative passages:

> Now to him who is able to strengthen you according
> to my gospel and the preaching of Jesus Christ, accord-

---

[27]For a discussion on this point see C. F. Evans, *Resurrection and the New Testament*, Studies in Biblical Theology, 2d series, 12 (London: SCM Press, 1970) 20ff. Matthew 27:53 reads: "and coming out of the tombs after his resurrection [μετὰ τὴν ἔγερσιν] they [the saints] went into the holy city and appeared to many."

[28]Gerhard Kittel, ed., *Theological Dictionary of the New Testament*, 10 vols. (Grand Rapids, Mich.: Eerdmans, 1964-1976) 3:335.

ing to the revelation of the mystery [κατὰ ἀποκάλυ-ψιν μυστηρίου] which was kept secret [σεσιγημέ-νου] for long ages, but is now disclosed [φανερω-θέντος δὲ νῦν] and through the prophetic writings is made known [γνωρισθέντος] to all nations, according to the command of the eternal God, to bring about the obedience of faith . . . (Rm 16:25-26)

. . . the mystery [τὸ μυστήριον] hidden for ages and generations but now made manifest [ἐφανερώθη] to his saints . . . (Col 1:26)

For he has made known [γνωρίσας] to us in all wisdom and insight the mystery of his will [τὸ μυστή-ριον τοῦ θελήματος αὐτοῦ], according to his purpose which he set forth in Christ as a plan for the fulness of time, to unite all things in him, things in heaven and things on earth . . . (Eph 1:9-10)

There are two common characteristics in all these texts: the word μυστήριον is always used in the singular, and it is linked with words denoting revelation, manifestation, making known, imparting or saying. In other words, the mystery is an open, revealed or manifested mystery. But although the mystery is now revealed and must be proclaimed, it still has an element that transcends human comprehension and reason. There is an ineffable quality to the mystery. The word mystery in the New Testament expresses the "drama of human redemption," the "drama of truth," in the words of Clement of Alexandria.[29] For St Paul, the mystery of God is Christ crucified (1 Cor 2:1-2), and this crucified Messiah is the incarnate Son of God, who is the goal of all creation (Eph 1:9-10). The term μυστήριον is firmly linked with the Christian kerygma and is never used by St Paul to refer to any cult, either Hellenistic or Christian.

The Christian μυστήριον has nothing in common with the μυστήρια of the Hellenistic cults. The Hellenistic

[29]See Rahner, 29.

μυστήρια (the plural form of the word, which appears most often in the records of the mystery cults but never in the New Testament) are not open or revealed but closed, unmanifested secrets. The revelation of the mystery referred to in the New Testament remains unknown in the mystery cults. The essential feature of the μυστήρια is precisely that they are never revealed. Thus, the different forms and applications of the term μυστήριον in the context of these two religious movements define the essential difference between them. The use of μυστήριον in Christian texts underlines the separation and difference from the mystery cults rather than any similarity to them, and cannot be due to the influence of the latter upon Christian origins.

When we come across concepts or images held in common by Christianity and the mystery cults, we must always be wary of explaining it as a borrowing. Some influential commentators ascribe every similarity between the New Testament faith and the cults strictly to the influence of the cults, which they regard as the rich supplier of important concepts and practices for this new religion. Yet others have seen these similarities in a different perspective that goes beyond the question of borrowing, and conclude that there are certain common elements found in both Christianity and the mysteries that neither borrowed from the other. These similarities came about in response to the deeper level of human nature and its needs. What is common in this case belongs to life as such, to the human condition. In some religious traditions these elements or practices are transformed into symbols, "the content and significance of which" in Christianity and the mystery cults are "entirely different."[30]

Death and the Soul in Christianity and in the Mysteries

The apparent resemblance between the dying and rising of Christ, on the one hand, and Attis, Adonis and Osiris, on the other, indicate no substantial agreement when examined in terms of their content. In the cults, the spirit of nature or of

[30]Ibid., 38.

vegetation dies and rises every year. Osiris, Attis and Adonis are mourned like mortals, and rejoicing follows the mourning. In Christ "all the fulness of God was pleased to dwell," and through him "all things, whether on earth or in heaven" were reconciled (Col 1:19-20). Christ is a historic person, not a force of nature. While death in the mystery cults means defeat, in the New Testament Christ's death is a victory, a triumph, the revelation of the glory of God. In the mysteries death is imposed on an unwilling god and his followers mourn him; in the New Testament the death of Christ is a voluntary one. In the mysteries the rising reverses the defeat of death; in the gospels the resurrection manifests what has been accomplished in a victorious death.[31] The death on the cross was a "resurrecting death." As the Easter hymn of the Orthodox Church proclaims: "Christ is risen from the dead, trampling down death by death, and upon those in the tomb bestowing life."

Very soon after the death and resurrection of Christ the Church expressed these events in the form of the credal statements of the kerygma (1 Cor 15:3ff). This and other early formulations of belief resulted from the concrete historical experience of Christ's death and resurrection and combined both historical data and theological meaning. Such formulations of doctrine were not used by the mystery cults or by the pagan religions. It was only in the latter part of the fourth century that Sallustius, a Roman pagan philosopher, attempted to produce an official codified catechism in response to questions raised in the philosophical movements and mystery cults

---

[31]"The sacrifice on the Cross is the climax from which any change would be an anticlimax," writes Arthur Darby Nock. The entire soteriological work of Christ is concentrated in this sacrifice, as is clear in the eucharistic prayer of the Hippolytan order, which is repeated in various liturgies:

> Who, when He was given over to His voluntary Passion, that He might break the bonds of death and rend the Devil's chains, and tread on Hell, and give light to the just, and fix bounds, and show His Resurrection . . .

Nock goes on to point out other differences between pagan and Christian resurrection, particularly the historical basis in Christianity, which is without parallel. See his *Early Gentile Christianity and its Hellenistic Background* (New York: Harper Torchbooks, 1964) 107. In his *Essays* Nock repeats the first point: "Attis, Adonis, Osiris die, are mourned for, and return to life. Yet it is nowhere said that *soteria* comes by their death." None of the dying vegetation deities died "for" other men (Nock, cited in Hengel, 25-6, n54).

of the period.[32] This is still far from a parallel to the apostolic
kerygma, in that there is no attempt to provide a historical
basis or offer historical evidence for pagan beliefs, but some of
its doctrines or attitudes point clearly to the separation of
Christian and pagan traditions.

Sallustius' treatise, for example, gives an explanation of
the pagan attitude toward the soul and its survival after death.
In the fourth part of the treatise, the soul is viewed as immortal
"because it knows the gods (and nothing mortal knows what
is immortal)." The soul and the body are two separate entities.
"The soul uses the body as an instrument, but is not within it,
just as the engineer is not within the engine." The fifth article
of faith goes on to state a belief in the transmigration of souls,
which is derived from the premise that "souls which are naturally qualified to act in the body must not, once they have left
it, remain inactive throughout time." Yet, unlike in the Hindu
tradition, "a rational soul could never become the soul of an
irrational creature."

This belief in an immortal soul which migrates to mortal
bodies differs radically from the biblical and Christian teachings. Christians regard the soul as not immortal by itself—it
is "not an independent or self-governing being, but precisely
a *creature,* and its very existence it owes to God, the Creator,"
who can make it immortal by his grace, emphasizes Georges
Florovsky.[33] From this Christian teaching about the soul we
see clearly that any theory of the transmigration of souls is
alien to the faith of the New Testament and the Church of the
fathers. The body is not divided from the soul. Man was created
for an eternal destiny, which is the resurrection of body and
soul. The patristic position is aptly summarized in Florovsky's
statement that Christians "are not committed to any philosophical doctrine of immortality. But they are committed to the
belief in general resurrection."[34]

[32]The text of this treatise, *Concerning the Gods and the Universe,* is given
in Frederick Grant, 179-96. It was meant to serve as an official catechism for
the Roman empire.

[33]Georges Florovsky, *Creation and Redemption,* Collected Works, 3 (Belmont, Mass.: Nordland, 1976) 216.

[34]Ibid., 239.

We may conclude that the Christian message of the resurrection of Christ does not correspond to anything in the Jewish and Hellenistic religious traditions and could not be derived from them. The accounts of the resurrection of Christ in the New Testament give us new material and new images to convey new happenings and a new experience. The newness comes from the very fact of revelation. The glory of the resurrected Christ has already appeared in history. The Christian hope of future salvation is now different from Jewish expectation. Salvation comes by the death and resurrection of Jesus and by individual incorporation into the body of the risen Messiah. This is also without parallel in the mystery religions, where the salvation of the believers does not depend upon the death and renewal of the gods. Where there is no real death there is no real resurrection, and thus there are no real parallels to the resurrection of Christ and its effects in the mystery cults. Whatever superficial similarities there may be among the religions of the Roman world, Christianity stands by itself, and its message of resurrection was not shaped by outside influences.

3

The Cross and the Tomb

Jesus was not a figure of mythology but of history. The events of his life belong to a definite, established period in human history. As the gospels chronicled the events of his life leading up to his passion and crucifixion, so they recorded his death and resurrection. His passion, death and resurrection were three decisive moments of his life. Without the narratives of the suffering and death, the accounts of the resurrection in the gospels cannot be understood. They are meant to be read and meditated on together, not in isolation from one another. We must never forget that those who told the story of his passion and death also witnessed and believed in his resurrection. The light of the resurrection illumines the utter limits of his suffering and the depths of his humiliation.

The story of the suffering of Jesus is told without emotion. Jesus is sinless, and he was unjustly treated. He proclaimed who he was before both the Jewish and the Roman authorities (Mk 14:61f, 15:2). His sufferings are those of the promised Messiah and the incarnate Son of God. "Obedient unto death, even death on a cross" (Ph 2:8), he put himself in the hands of his Father. This is the story of the divine Son handed over to death. By putting him on the cross his executioners exercised their power to the utmost, demonstrating their seemingly complete authority yet at the same time the limit of it. At this very moment the power, authority and glory of God was manifested, for the death of Christ was not a defeat but a victory. As his burial confirmed his death, so the empty tomb was the sign of what the Father willed for him: a "life-creating death." Christ's death points to his resurrection.

The primitive Church, in its proclamation, the kerygma, taught that his death was for the salvation of man. He died "for our sins in accordance with the scriptures" (1 Cor 15:3). The passion accounts of the gospels are full of references to the figure of the righteous sufferer of the Old Testament, indicating that the events described in the story of Christ's suffering correspond to the plan of God for the salvation of mankind. Christ is himself the victor over death, which he robbed of its power. The resurrection demonstrated this destruction of death. "How could the destruction of death have been manifested at all, had not the Lord's body been raised?" asks St Athanasius.[1] The death and resurrection of Christ are for the salvation of man, St Paul asserts—they are two phases of the one decisive event of salvation. He "was put to death for our trespasses and raised for our justification" (Rm 4:25). The death and resurrection are inseparable as events of salvation.

The Hour of Darkness

The hour of the death of Christ is the hour of darkness. All three synoptics mention darkness occurring at the moment of his death: "And when the sixth hour had come, there was darkness over the whole land until the ninth hour" (Mk 15:33; also Mt 27:45 and Lk 23:44). The "whole land" or, as we find in Matthew, "all the land" that is overcome by darkness is probably Judea, which symbolically may stand for the whole of creation. This is a constant theme in the Holy Friday services of the Orthodox Church:

> When Thou wast crucified, O Christ, all the creation
> saw and trembled. The foundations of the earth quaked
> in fear of Thy power. The lights of heaven hid them-
> selves and the veil of the temple was rent in twain; the
> mountains trembled and the rocks were split.

[1]Athanasius, *On the Incarnation,* tr. and ed. A Religious of C.S.M.V., introduction by C. S. Lewis (Crestwood, N.Y.: SVS Press, 1980) 60.

The whole creation was changed by fear, when it saw Thee, O Christ, hanging on the Cross. The sun was darkened and the foundations of the earth were shaken; all things suffered with the Creator of all. Of Thine own will Thou hast endured this for our sakes.[2]

During the Vespers of Holy Friday the faithful sing again that when Christ was hanging upon the cross "all things suffered with the Creator of all." Creation "suffers, seeing the Lord crucified." It was a strange wonder "to behold the Creator of heaven and earth hanging upon the Cross. The sun was darkened and the day was changed again to night."[3] The iconography of the Orthodox Church also shows the light of both the sun and moon darkened in the scene of Golgotha.

The evangelists refer to the phenomenon of darkness as apparently occurring in time and space, as a natural phenomenon. Yet they did not see natural causes as the principal reason for the darkness that accompanied the crucifixion and death of Christ. For the evangelists and for the early Church, the one who was lifted up and who died on the cross was not simply a man but the Messiah, the Son of God or the Son of Man. In the Holy Friday hymns of the Church he is "the master of creation," "the releaser of Adam" or "the destroyer of hell." The one who loves mankind is "nailed to the cross that he may release the prisoners of hell." Whatever the "natural" reasons for the darkness might have been, we should keep in mind that the darkening of the sun and moon and earthquakes are linked in the Bible with the coming of the Day of the Lord. Thus, for New Testament Christians these phenomena are signs that the cross of Christ is the fulfilment of the scriptures, that the Day of the Lord has come.

The evangelist John is the only one who does not connect the death of Christ with this strange occurrence of darkness. He does, however, mention darkness just before the hour of Christ's glorification. When Judas took the morsel of bread

---

[2]Matins of Holy Friday, verses on the Beatitudes and the aposticha, in Mother Mary and Archimandrite Kallistos Ware, trs. and eds., *Lenten Triodion* (London: Faber and Faber, 1978) 590, 598.
[3]Verses on "Lord, I have Cried," ibid., 611.

and immediately went out, St John pointedly records "and it was night" (13:30). It was "night," darkness, both in the physical, natural sense and in the spiritual sense. The Last Supper, being the Passover meal, could have begun only after the sun had set. This is the physical aspect of "night" (νύξ). This was a special night, the night of the betrayal by Judas.

It was also "night" in a profound spiritual connotation. St John displays particular interest in the image of darkness in his gospel, using this image more than any of the synoptic writers. In his prologue he writes: "In him was life, and the life was the light of men. The light shines in the darkness, and the darkness has not overcome it" (1:4-5). Here "darkness" stands for the powers of evil, which cannot defeat the very life and goodness that comes from God. The life and the light that came into the world represent judgment (ἡ κρίσις), for "men loved darkness [τὸ σκότος] rather than light, because their deeds were evil" (3:19). The crucifixion and death of Christ are the judgment of this world, and the death of Christ breaks the dominion of Satan over men (12:31f). In the last discourse Christ tells his disciples: "I will no longer talk much with you, for the ruler of this world is coming. He has no power over me" (14:30). The power of darkness proves powerless.

Accordingly, St John goes beyond the synoptics, linking the theme of darkness not only with the suffering and death of Christ but also with his incarnation, with the very coming of the incarnate Son of God. Those who reject the gift of God, the Son whom he sent and gave for the salvation of mankind, find themselves in darkness. On Golgotha Christ triumphed in glory—he is the light in the darkness. And for anyone who sees the revealed glory of God, which illumines all things, there is no darkness. St John, it seems, is less interested in the physical phenomenon of darkness than in its spiritual meaning.[4] Yet he does not ignore the physical aspect of the fact of darkness, just as the first three evangelists, as we have already indicated, do not overlook its spiritual aspect.

---

[4]See U. Holzmeister, "Die Finsternis beim Tode Jesu," *Biblica* 22 (1941) 404-16.

The Seven Words from the Cross

The gospels record various sayings spoken by Christ just before his death. The first two evangelists—St Matthew and St Mark—give us one saying, St Luke gives three others and St John adds three sayings that belong to his tradition. Altogether we possess seven different pronouncements from the cross.

There is no indisputable basis to be found in the gospels for arranging these seven sayings of the crucified Christ in a definite chronological order. We can construct a possible chronological order, however, by ascribing some of these sayings to the beginning of the suffering of Christ on the cross and others to the end, just before his death. To the first group we can assign Luke 23:34 and 23:43 along with John 19:26-27, and in the second we shall place Mark 15:34 (Mt 27:46), John 19:28 and 19:30 and Luke 23:46. We will discuss the pronouncements in this order.[5] What is certain about these words from the cross is that they are all expressions of fulfilment. The messianic mission is completed. These words recall for us the Old Testament promise, as well as the words and works of Christ during his public ministry.

With the words from Luke 23:34, "Father, forgive them; for they know not what they do," which may be taken as the first words spoken on the cross, Jesus reveals the mystery of the cross. Christ is the one who brings heaven and earth together. The cross is the source and the foundation of the gospel of forgiveness. With these words Christ was praying both for the Jews and for the gentiles, who actively participated in and bore responsibility for his death sentence. They could not claim ignorance—they needed forgiveness. Enough had been revealed to enable them to see that Jesus was innocent, and yet they unjustly condemned him. In return, he asks that they may experience the mercy of the Father. Before the crucifixion his persecutors had the power to release or condemn him,

---

[5]See also Karl Rahner's order of exposition in his *Watch and Pray with Me: The Seven Last Words* (New York: Seabury Press, 1966) 49ff. He starts with Lk 23:34, followed by Lk 23:43, Jn 19:26-27, Mt 27:46, Jn 19:28, 19:30, and Lk 23:46.

and they decided to condemn him. With this final act their power and authority was itself condemned, and the power of forgiveness was released. The words of Christ are also the acts of Christ, and these words are fully congruous with his forgiveness of sinners during his public ministry. Christ on the cross does not wait for the repentance of his executioners; he does not expect them to be moved by his suffering. Instead, he offers them forgiveness while they still remain in their sins. In this Jesus goes beyond the attitude of the Pharisees, who would approach and accept only a repentant sinner.[6]

These words of Jesus about forgiveness have an interesting history. Some Christian scribes who copied the Gospel of St Luke during the time of the Christian-Jewish disputes and antagonisms betrayed their feelings by omitting Luke 23:34 in their manuscripts. They assumed that Christ could not have forgiven those leading authorities who put him to death. Yet those who followed him before and after his resurrection imitated his example by asking forgiveness for their enemies. The martyr Stephen, for example, while he was being stoned, "knelt down and cried with a loud voice, 'Lord, do not hold this sin against them' " (Acts 7:60).

The first fruit of the forgiveness from the cross was the repentance of one of the two criminals who were crucified with Christ, one on his left side and one on his right. One railed at him; the other asked the crucified Messiah to remember him in his kingdom. To this petition Jesus responded with the words: "Truly, I say to you, today you will be with me in Paradise" (Lk 23:43). After his death Jesus promises him paradise. The emphasis in this saying is upon the word "today" (σήμερον), upon the present, and upon "with me" (μετ' ἐμοῦ). Christ's death will change many things. It is not enough that the repentant criminal will be in proximity to Jesus—he will be granted "to eat of the tree of life, which is in the paradise of God" (Rv 2:7). To be in paradise, the place where God dwells, is

---

[6]For the view that these words, in whichever order we take them, are related to the public ministry of Christ, see Karl Rahner, 49f. See also Thorleif Boman, "Das letzte Wort Jesu," *Studia Theologica* 17:2 (1963) 103-19; and John Wilkinson, "The Seven Words from the Cross," *Scottish Journal of Theology* 17:1 (1964) 69-82.

to be "under the altar" of God (Rv 6:9ff). The word paradise
is Persian for garden, the place man lost after the fall. With
his death on the cross Christ recalls the first creation, he restores
the relations with God that were broken with the fall of Adam.
Paradise is the destiny of the righteous. Those who experience
the forgiveness and salvation that comes from God are in the
presence of God. Everything is going to be different after his
death—"today" is the first day of the new creation. This is the
meaning of the second saying from the cross.

To be with Christ is to share a common life, one which has
already begun for all those who "have been raised with Christ"
and who "seek the things that are above, where Christ is, seated
at the right hand of God" (Col 3:1). The third saying points to
this life in common, the common life in the body of Christ,
which is the Church. At the cross of Jesus stood his mother
and the beloved disciple. He said to his mother: "Woman,
behold your son!" And to the disciple he said: "Behold, your
mother!" And "from that hour the disciple took her to his own
home," as St John records (19:26-27). Patristic and modern
interpreters of the fourth gospel have devoted much attention
to the meaning of these words as well as of this entire scene.
In most interpretations the beloved disciple represents the
ideal Christian, while Mary at the foot of the cross stands for
the new Eve ("Woman"!), the spiritual mother of all the
faithful, who now have Mary for their mother. Mary also
stands symbolically for the Church. Thus, the motherhood of
the Church and the sonship of the believers are proclaimed
from the cross.

The words from the cross that have represented particular
difficulties for many Christians throughout the centuries are
the ones of suffering and distress: "My God, my God, why
have you forsaken me?" (Mk 15:34; Mt 27:46) Scholars are
divided over the question of the language in which Jesus uttered
these words. Was it in Aramaic, the spoken language of the
time, or classical Hebrew? Some argue forcefully that Christ
used a Hebrew form of the saying. This argument is based on
the comment of the bystanders who, after hearing these words,
said "Behold, he is calling Elijah" (Mk 15:35). There was a
popular belief that the prophet Elijah would come to the rescue

of the pious. The remark of the bystanders would be understandable, then, if Jesus cried with a loud voice "ἠλεὶ ἠλεὶ"
or "ἠλὶ ἠλὶ" (Eli, Eli), as is reported in Matthew 27:46,
rather than the "Ἐλωΐ" (Eloi) we find in Mark 15:34, which
is an Aramaic form.[7] There is no disagreement, however, that
these words are the opening words of Psalm 22.

Psalm 22 is the prayer of the righteous sufferer. In it the
righteous sufferer is "scorned by men, and despised by the
people" (22:6), he is encircled by a company of evildoers who
behave toward him like savage animals. They "have pierced
my hands and feet," and "divide my garments among them,
and for my raiment they cast lots" (22:16, 18). Yet the righteous sufferer is not in despair, for he hopes in the Lord and his
salvation: "O Lord, be not far off! O thou my help, hasten to
my aid! Deliver my soul from the sword, my life from the
power of the dog [enemy]!" (22:19-20) He will praise the
name of the Lord. The psalm ends with a clear expression of
hope: "Posterity shall serve him; men shall tell of the Lord
to the coming generation, and proclaim his deliverance to a
people yet unborn, that he has wrought it" (22:30-31). Only if
the opening verse of the psalm is taken by itself, without any
consideration of what follows, is there a possibility of interpreting it as an expression of despair.

The early Church would never have ascribed to Christ the
words of Psalm 22:1 if he had not uttered them himself. We
may also assume that he did not recite only the first verse of
the psalm but continued with the rest. Brought up in a pious
Jewish household, he used to recite the Psalms, the main part
of the Jewish prayerbook. We may assume that the rest of the

---

[7]Vincent Taylor, *The Gospel according to St. Mark* (London: Macmillan,
1959) 592ff.

All this debate over whether the words of Christ on the cross reported in
Matthew 27:46, *"Eli, Eli, lama sabachthani,"* are in Hebrew or Aramaic, or
half Hebrew and half Aramaic, may finally be brought to an end, says Joseph
A. Fitzmyer in "The Aramaic Language and the Study of the New Testament,"
Journal of Biblical Literature 99:1 (1980) 5-21. A newly discovered Palestinian Aramaic text, not yet published but widely known to Aramaic experts,
preserves the use of *el* as a name for God in Aramaic, in contrast to the usual
elah(a). "Even though the Aramaic suffixal form *eli* has not yet turned up, the
absolute *el*, 'God,' turns up several times in this text."

psalm, repeated in a weak voice, was lost in the noise and chaotic atmosphere that accompanied the crucifixion.

As we have already pointed out, the fact that Christ spoke these words from Psalm 22 when he was on the cross have perplexed many pious Christians for centuries. Some modern existentialist interpreters find a way out of this perplexity by seeing in these words an expression of the despair of the human condition, of loss of hope and utter loneliness in the universe. John P. Meier, however, responds that we "can safely ignore" the modern existentialist interpretation of these words as words of despair. The righteous sufferer is in anguish and complains aloud, yet his lament only demonstrates his "close sense of intimacy" and trust toward God. "He is on such intimate terms with God that he can voice his complaint in no uncertain terms." The harshness of the complaint is intended to arouse God to save the just man, who knows his cry will be heard and whose cry is answered by the apocalyptic occurrences at the time of Christ's death and by his resurrection. Thus, the words of Jesus "bespeak both his real anguish and his filial trust in the Father."[8] Karl Rahner meditates on these words in the following manner:

> To express Your anguish . . . You began to say the twenty-second psalm . . . the only prayer that You wanted to say during this most bitter agony was one that had been prayed thousands and thousands of years ago. In a sense You prayed in the words of the liturgy when You offered Your own solemn Mass, that Mass in which You offered Yourself as an eternal sacrifice.[9]

More than this, the fathers of the Church saw that the passion of Christ invested Psalm 22 with a new meaning. They noted that Christ had passed through all the sufferings of human beings whose sin separates them from God. The sinner has abandoned God and "loved darkness rather than light" (Jn 3:19). The climax of this estrangement of man from God

[8]John P. Meier, *The Vision of Matthew: Christ, Church and Morality in the First Gospel* (New York: Paulist Press, 1979) 203-4.

[9]Karl Rahner, 49f.

finds its full expression when Christ cries out "My God, my God, why have you forsaken me?" He speaks these words in the name of humanity, to bring an end to alienation and to turn the face of man toward God, who has been searching for him. In union with God and solidarity with man, Christ turns man toward his God. He prays that the Father may look upon us, for he took on all of our nature except sin when he became man. On account of the disobedience of Adam we were all separated from God and left alone, to the prey of evil powers. But now, with the cry of Christ from the cross, we are accepted and saved, as St Athanasius and many others proclaimed. Christ on the cross is not abandoned by the Father. In his person he represents us, and is praying on our behalf.

None of these interpretations have any intention of minimizing the real suffering of Christ. On the contrary, the fathers see his suffering as the starting and essential point in their interpretation, while at the same time they stress the mystery of the incarnate God dying on the cross. The point is that there is no room in the New Testament account for any interpretation of faithlessness, loneliness or despair. Modern exegetes warn us constantly that we must study Old Testament quotations or allusions in the New Testament in their various contexts. Only in the context of the psalm as a whole, as well as in the context of all the events of Christ's saving passion, can we arrive at an adequate interpretation of these words of Christ from the cross. Christ on the cross experienced the most extreme form of suffering and distress, but not despair.[10] And with the words of the psalmist he proclaimed his ultimate trust in the deliverance of God for all mankind which suffers on account of sin.

St John does not record the words of Psalm 22:1 in his gospel, but the two additional sayings he does give in his passion account illumine the meaning of the words recorded in Mark and Matthew. The sayings St John records are "I thirst" and "It is finished" (19:28 and 30). The words "I thirst" point

[10]See Pierre Benoit, *The Passion and Resurrection of Jesus Christ* (New York: Herder and Herder, 1969). Benoit writes that "distress is the word we should use, not despair. Despair presupposes the loss of confidence in God, distress implies only an enormous sadness and desolation" (194-5).

first of all to the physical suffering of Christ, and their deeper
meaning should never exclude their literal sense. Any spiritual
meaning is not a substitute for the literal, physical meaning, but
includes and goes beyond it. On one level the words "I thirst"
express the suffering of Christ, and on another level they indicate that the real purpose and goal of his suffering and death
is to return to the Father. To understand the full impact of
these words, we again have to go back to the Psalms:

> My soul thirsts for God, for the living God.
> When shall I come and behold the face of God? (42:2)

> O God, thou art my God, I seek thee, my soul thirsts
>   for thee;
> my flesh faints for thee, as in a dry and weary land
>   where no water is. (63:1)

> They gave me poison for food, and for my thirst they
>   gave me vinegar to drink. (69:21)

While the first two verses speak undoubtedly about spiritual
thirst, the thirst for God, the last one expresses the need to
satisfy physical thirst. Jesus comes from the Father and by way
of death goes back to the Father, for whom he has "thirsted."
His life is a journey, which will be completed with the resurrection and the ascension.

With the expression "It is finished" we are called to remember the "High-priestly Prayer" before the crucifixion (Jn 17).
Here Jesus addresses the Father: "I am coming to thee" (17:11,
13). With the words "It is finished" his journey reaches its
goal. Christ attains the end in love and obedience to the will
of the Father. "It is finished" (τετέλεσται) means "it is
completed." But this end also means, however, the beginning
of the new level of existence. The last words of Christ from
the cross in the fourth gospel are words not of defeat but of
triumph and victory.

The third recorded saying of Jesus in Luke—the last words
from the cross in our order of discussion—indicates yet again

the absolute confidence of the crucified Messiah in his Father. With the words "Father, into thy hands I commit my spirit" (Lk 23:46) Jesus expresses his intimacy, his confidence in his union with the Father as well as in the knowledge that his life and messianic work have reached τέλος, completion. In the gospels, only Christ pronounces the word "abba," "father." He died with words of prayer (cf Ps 31:5).

The words from the cross differ from one gospel to another. Of the seven, only one saying is recorded by two evangelists (Mk 15:34 and Mt 27:46). Yet all of these words are words of revelation that tell us about Christ and his work. When death was imminent, Jesus maintained and illumined with these sayings the character of his teaching and activity. They become clearer and more vivid at the very end than they ever could have been before.

The Death of Christ

The moment of the death of Jesus is depicted with a slightly different expression in each of the gospels. St Matthew writes that Jesus "yielded up his spirit" (ἀφῆκεν τὸ πνεῦμα, 27:50). This choice of words points to a transition or transformation at the moment of his death. His life goes beyond the end of this earthly existence. This way of describing his death is similar to that of John 19:30, where Jesus "bowed his head and gave up his spirit [παρέδωκεν τὸ πνεῦμα]." The words used in Matthew—ἀφίημι—and John—παραδίδωμι—bring out the fact that the death of Christ is a voluntary death, as the fathers have noted. This voluntary character of his death also belongs to the gospels as a whole: "I lay down my life, that I may take it again. No one takes it from me, but I lay it down of my own accord" (Jn 10:17-18).

St Mark records that "Jesus uttered a loud cry, and breathed his last [ἐξέπνευσεν]" (15:37), and St Luke adds to the words we have already discussed—"Father, into thy hands I commit my spirit [παρατίθεμαι τὸ πνεῦμα μου]"— "having said this he breathed his last [ἐξέπνευσεν]" (23:46). These two evangelists use the verb ἐκπνέω, which means to expire and which also connotes a voluntary death. The account in Mark appears to be the most expressive. Jesus cries aloud and expires. His death is the death of the suffering Messiah who at the moment of expiring accomplishes his mission.

Whatever terms they use, the gospel writers all emphasize that the death of Jesus is not an ordinary death. All four evangelists see it as a voluntary death, and all four avoid using the ordinary verbs for dying (ἀποθνήσκω or τελευτάω) to describe it. His death was an extraordinary event. One commentator has characterized his last cry as recorded in Mark as "a shout of victory, presaging the resurrection."[11] Christ's death was not a defeat that would be recovered only on the following Sunday morning, but rather is itself a moment of victory in the history of our salvation. Moreover, this significance of the death of Christ was noted in the earliest account of the crucifixion. As C. H. Dodd has said, if ever there "was a time when the Church could think of the cross only as a disaster retrieved by the resurrection, and that only subsequent reflection found positive meaning in it," then "it is a period to which we have no access."[12]

In the earliest traditions recorded in the New Testament, Jesus is portrayed as one who in his life of perfect obedience to the Father fulfilled the role of the Suffering Servant of the Lord (see, for example, Is 52:13-53:12) and who died for the salvation of "many." He poured out his life for many (Mk 14:24) —"one" dies for "many."

The meaning of this "many" for whom Christ's work is accomplished has caused some problems for interpreters. The three main passages in which it occurs are Mark 10:45 ("For the Son of man also came not to be served but to serve, and to give his life as a ransom for many"), the words of institution in Mark 14:24 and Matthew 26:28 ("This is my blood of the covenant, which is poured out for many") and Hebrews 9:28 ("so Christ, having been offered once to bear the sins of many, will appear a second time"). Most interpreters agree that

[11]David M. Stanley, *Faith and Religious Life: A New Testament Perspective* (New York: Paulist Press, 1971) 11.
[12]C. H. Dodd, *According to the Scriptures: The Sub-Structure of New Testament Theology* (New York: Charles Scribner's Sons, 1953) 123.

"many" does not express a limitation on the universal character of the death of Christ, that he died only for some rather than for all. And among many scholars we find the view expressed that the phrase "for many" represents merely a Semitic idiom for "for all."

C.F.D. Moule, however, is skeptical of this interpretation, insisting that "for many" is meant to underline the extraordinary results of Christ's sacrifice on the cross. The real point is in the contrast between "one" and "many"—one deed accomplishes a plurality of results, exactly as in Romans 5:12ff. The "many" serves "to emphasize the remarkable fruitfulness of the one act of self-surrender."[13] Through his death as a sacrifice to God, the solidarity between Christ and the "many" has been made most personal—by baptism now we are "united with him in a death like his" (Rm 6:5).

From the beginning of the Christian tradition, the death of Christ has been seen as something much more than just a moral act of obedience and love. For the New Testament writers his death is a free gift, a sacrifice, an offering to God. The words of the high-priestly prayer "And for their sake I consecrate myself" (Jn 17:19) were paraphrased by St John Chrysostom as "I offer thee a sacrifice" for their sake. God accepted this pure sacrifice, and thus St Peter could write to the Christians in Asia Minor: "You know that you were ransomed from the futile ways inherited from your fathers, not with perishable things such as silver or gold, but with the precious blood of Christ, like that of a lamb without blemish or spot" (1 Pet 1:18-19). St Paul exhorts the Christians in Ephesus to walk in love, "as Christ loved us and gave himself up for us, a fragrant offering and sacrifice to God" (Eph 5:2). According to the author of Hebrews, this sacrifice has its beginning in the passion and the cross and finds its completion in God—through the veil of his flesh Christ entered the tabernacle of God (Hb 10:19-20). To enter the sanctuary is to enter the glory. With the acceptance of the sacrifice Jesus was transformed from

---

[13]C. F. D. Moule, *The Origin of Christology* (Cambridge, England: University Press, 1977) 119f.

earthly existence to the sphere of the heavenly, sacred, transcendent existence.[14]

The fourth evangelist records how "one of the soldiers pierced his side with a spear, and at once there came out blood and water" (Jn 19:34). This is an account of what actually happened, yet at the same time it points beyond itself. In the minds of St John and the early Church, it symbolically indicates that his death is the source of life for "many," that baptism and the eucharist are rooted in the death and resurrection of Christ.

The Burial of Christ

The crucifixion was watched by "all his acquaintances and the women who had followed him from Galilee," who "stood at a distance and saw these things" (Lk 23:49; cf Mt 27:55-56; Mk 15:40-41; and Jn 19:25-27). They also watched the burial of Jesus. All four evangelists record that it was not one of his disciples, however, but Joseph of Arimathea, "a respected member of the council" (Mk 15:43), who took courage, went to Pilate and asked for the body of Jesus (Mt 27:58; Mk 15:43; Lk 23:52; Jn 19:38). The story of the burial of Jesus is firmly linked with the name of Joseph of Arimathea, and there is no reason not to accept it as recorded.[15] Joseph laid Jesus in a new tomb (Jn 19:41-42 and parallels) and the "women who had come with him from Galilee followed, and saw the tomb, and how his body was laid" (Lk 23:55 and parallels). Here we have witnesses to the burial of Jesus and a record of how he was buried, where and by whom.

[14]For an excellent discussion on the sacrifice of Christ, see F. X. Durrwell, *The Resurrection: A Biblical Study* (New York: Sheed and Ward, 1960) 59-77.

[15]There was room for compassion in Roman practice, and the authorities would sometimes hand over the body of an executed criminal to friends or relatives. Archeologists have uncovered the skeletal remains of a young man who had been crucified not long after the time of Christ in a family tomb north of Jerusalem, which demonstrates that it was possible, though not at all normal, for a crucified body to receive an honorable burial. See G. O'Collins, *The Easter Jesus* (London: Darton, Longman and Todd, 1973) 39-40; see also the articles by V. Tzaferis and N. Haas in the *Israel Exploration Journal* 20 (1970) 18-32, 38-59.

Christ's burial underlines the reality of his death and reflects the Jewish burial customs of his time. The law demands the burial of all the dead, even of criminals or rebels, and even of those who suffered death on a cross. Burial had to be performed before sunset, as is well known. Jesus died on Friday afternoon and was left on the cross a short time before being buried on this Friday, before sunset. His body was buried before the beginning of the new day, which in this case was the Sabbath. According to the Gospel of St John, that Sabbath was "a day of special solemnity" or "a high day" (this is how the Jerusalem Bible and the RSV respectively translate the μεγάλη ἡ ἡμέρα of Jn 19:31). This expression probably indicates that it was the day of Passover. But whether or not Passover fell on the Sabbath in the year of the death of Jesus, Jewish law forbade leaving a dead body unburied during any Sabbath. Moreover, the bodies of those who had died on a cross were considered contaminated and therefore could not normally be buried in the family tomb, which must remain undefiled. There was nothing in the Jewish law, however, to prevent the body of an executed man from being buried in a new tomb if one was available. Otherwise, the bodies of condemned rebels or criminals were buried in a common tomb. Jesus was buried in a new tomb by a man whose name has been preserved in all four gospels. They record one burial, one tomb, and a man of reputation, Joseph of Arimathea, who performed this final act.

Curiously, in modern times a theory of two burials of Jesus has appeared, apparently in an effort to cast doubt on the veracity of the accounts that the tomb was found empty. The critics who hold to this theory need to explain away the testimony and facts related to Christ's burial in order to undermine the historicity of the whole sequence of events leading to the resurrection. One such account of two burials was published in 1932 by G. Baldensperger.[16] According to his hypothesis, Jesus was buried first in a common grave with those who were crucified with him. The women who accompanied him watched this burial, and on the morning of the first day of the week they

---

[16] G. Baldensperger, "Le tombeau vide," in *Revue d'Histoire et de Philosophie Religieuses* 12 (1932); 13 (1933); 14 (1934), summarized and evaluated in Benoit, 229-30.

visited this common grave but did not find the body of Jesus in it. On this basis they asserted that the tomb was found empty. However, this was because a second burial had occurred, according to this theory, a private burial after the first one and after all the witnesses had gone away. Baldensperger surmises that Joseph of Arimathea asked for and got permission from the Roman authorities to carry the body of Jesus from the common grave into a new tomb, and no one was present to witness this transfer.

We must admire the imaginativeness of this theory, but of course there is no evidence for such a speculation. Our only sources furnish no basis whatsoever for a theory of two burials. When the resurrection was proclaimed in Jerusalem, both the disciples and their opponents accepted the fact of one burial in one tomb, which was found empty. This discovery they explained differently, however. The disciples saw the empty tomb as a sign of the resurrection, whereas the enemies of Jesus claimed that the body was stolen (see Mt 28:11-15). Pierre Benoit, the well-known New Testament scholar who has lived in Palestine for a long time and who is well acquainted with Jewish laws and customs, gives the following appraisal of the "two-burial theory": Baldensperger's "knowledge is bookish and unreal, and the romance he offers us cannot shake the solidly based narrative of the Gospel." He introduces a long period between the first and second burial, but "there is no room for more than one burial."[17]

In addition to the gospel accounts, the burial of Christ is included in the early Christian kerygma (1 Cor 15:4) and is referred to in the apostolic sermon on the day of Pentecost (Acts 2:27-31). These are the earliest written records of the received tradition concerning the death of Jesus, our closest direct link with the event itself.

The Descent into Hades

Christ died on the cross, but he could not remain in death. Even in his death he continued his redemptive work. At the

[17]Ibid.

moment of death the evangelists Matthew and Mark narrate that "the curtain of the temple was torn in two" (Mt 27:51; Mk 15:38). They probably have in mind the curtain that separates the Holy of Holies from the Holy Place of the temple, which stood as a symbol of separation between God and man. The death of Jesus opened the way into the Holy of Holies, into the presence of God, for all people. With his voluntary death on the cross Christ "has broken down the dividing wall of hostility" between God and man and brought an end to their enmity and estrangement (Eph 2:14ff). God and man are reconciled and united on account of his death.

The words of St Matthew that immediately follow his statement about the rending of the curtain may be interpreted as a dramatic description of Christ's descent into Hades: "and the earth shook, and the rocks were split; the tombs also were opened, and many of the bodies of the saints who had fallen asleep were raised, and coming out of the tombs after his resurrection they went into the holy city and appeared to many" (Mt 27:51-53). St Matthew also mentions an earthquake in 28:2, thus connecting the death and resurrection of Christ. This earthquake is a sign of revelation, of theophany. It underlines the importance of these events, the decisive moment in the history of salvation, the point at which a crucial decision must be made for the present and the future. The meaning of the death and resurrection of Christ can be adequately grasped only if they are linked together and never contemplated in isolation from one another. The earthquake, a sign of God's revelation, points to the death on the cross as a victory and not a defeat. The resurrection revealed and sealed what had been accomplished on the cross. Christ on the cross and Christ in the tomb is the victor, not the victim.

St Matthew goes on in the rest of this passage to again emphasize the nexus between the cross and the resurrection. The holy city where the saints appear should be understood as the heavenly Jerusalem instead of the earthly Jerusalem. With vivid apocalyptic imagery, Matthew conveys the meaning and the consequences of the death of Christ. Those who were in

Sheol are freed, and the final age has started.[18] The tombs that were opened signify once more that the Day of the Lord has arrived, that the kingdom of God has been inaugurated. Like the tearing of the curtain, the raising of the Old Testament saints reveals the purpose of the coming of Christ. The hour of his death is a time of deliverance.

Georges Florovsky has called the cross of Christ a "resurrecting cross" and his death a "resurrecting death." The resurrecting Christ descended into Hades, "not in humiliation although through humiliation," and delivered the captives.[19] Christ descends into Sheol in his glory, and "the gospel was preached even to the dead" (καὶ νεκροῖς εὐηγγελίσθη, 1 Pet 4:6). His death was a real death, which like any other death of a human being consisted of separation of the soul from the body. Yet in his death his body and soul remained in a binding personal relationship in the divine person of the Logos who became man.[20] This point is brought out quite clearly in Orthodox worship, in the Liturgy of Preparation:

In the tomb with the body; in Hell with the soul, as God; in Paradise with the thief; and on the throne with the Father and the Spirit wast Thou, O Christ, filling all things, Thyself uncircumscribed.

On Holy Saturday the Church also commemorates the mystery of the descent of Christ into Hades, contemplating the cross and the descent together in the economy of salvation: "Uplifted

[18]Donald Senior, "The Death of Jesus and the Resurrection of the Holy Ones," *Catholic Biblical Quarterly* 38 (1976) 312-29. Commenting on Mt 27:52-53, John P. Meier writes: "The earthquake is not an isolated sign . . . [it] splits the rocks, the splitting of the rocks opens the sepulchers, and the opening of the sepulchers permits the dead to come forth. One could not imagine a more striking—and daring—symbol of the truth that the death of Christ *is* the eschatological event, which includes the general resurrection." Meier goes on to say that the resurrection of all that was prophesied by Ezekiel (37:1-14) takes place "proleptically" here (34).

[19]Georges Florovsky, "On the Tree of the Cross," *St. Vladimir's Seminary Quarterly* 1:3-4 (1953) 20f.

[20]On this point see my article "Hypostatic and Prosopic Union in the Exegesis of Christ's Temptation," *St. Vladimir's Seminary Quarterly* 9:3 (1965) 118-37.

on the Cross, Thou hast uplifted with Thyself all living
men; and then descending beneath the earth, Thou raisest all
that lie buried there."[21] In another hymn, Christ destroys the
door of Hades so that it cannot be used anymore. He does not
knock on this door—he destroys it. The very death of Christ
manifests life: "O happy tomb! It received within itself the
Creator as one asleep, and it was made a divine treasury of
life."[22]

The unity between the cross and the resurrection that we
see in the gospels and in the liturgical and dogmatic tradition
of the Church is also vividly expressed in the iconography of
the Church. The crucified Christ is pictured with his head
bowed toward his mother Mary, who stands at the foot of the
cross with the apostle John. His eyes are closed; he looks as one
"asleep." His sufferings are real, but his face is not distorted.
His whole body bears an expression of majesty in suffering, as
if the last enemy—death—is powerless to destroy this man on
the cross. The icon bears witness to his suffering and death—
he is subject to all this, but not to corruption. This crucifixion
icon has been described as "the concrete expression of Christian
mystery, of victory by defeat, of glory by humiliation, of life
by death," and precisely in this is the Christian mystery: that
the resurrection is already present in the death of Christ.[23] The
"hour" of the cross is the moment when Christ revealed who
he is. The spiritual history of mankind finds its center and
dividing line in this hour. Up to this moment mankind knew
only the power of death and corruption; it was alienated from
God. But with this "hour" Christ, the head of the new humanity who has overcome death by death, is lifted up and made
known to "many." The icon of the crucifixion is an icon of
revelation.

There is a transition, a gradual passing of "a day of rever-
ent silence and expectation," on Holy Friday, into a day of

[21]From the "Praises" of Holy Saturday Matins, in Mary and Ware, 627.

[22]From the canon in Holy Saturday Matins, ode 7, in ibid., 650.

[23]For a discussion of this icon, see Leonid Ouspensky and Vladimir Lossky,
The Meaning of Icons (Boston, 1952) 183-4. See also Vladimir Lossky, *Orthodox Theology: An Introduction* (Crestwood, N.Y.: SVS Press, 1978) 117-8,
for the theological implications discussed here. The icon is reproduced in
plate 2.

joy, which is the day of resurrection. The two-natured grain of wheat which had been sown on Friday in the bosom of the earth shattered the bars of Hades, drove away its darkness, released Adam and on Sunday brought joy to the world. Even during the most joyous of all Orthodox feasts, whenever the Church relives the resurrection in worship, the cross of Christ is not forgotten:

> Having beheld the Resurrection of Christ, let us worship the holy Lord Jesus, the only Sinless One. We venerate thy cross, O Christ, and thy holy Resurrection we praise and glorify; for thou art our God, and we know no other than thee; we call on thy name. Come all you faithful, let us venerate Christ's holy Resurrection. For, behold, through the cross joy has come into all the world. Ever blessing the Lord, let us praise his Resurrection. By enduring the cross for us, he destroyed death by death.[24]

---

[24]Resurrection hymn sung at the Sunday Matins service.

4

The Empty Tomb on the Third Day

All four gospels attest to the death and burial of Christ, as we have just seen in the preceding chapter. All four also record the visit of the women to the tomb of Christ on "the first day of the week." They probably went "to see the sepulcher" (Mt 28:1) and to mourn, although Mark says that they planned to anoint the body of Jesus, already two nights in the tomb. No idea of resurrection entered their minds. When they reached the sepulcher, the large stone from the door of the tomb had been rolled back, and entering the tomb they saw "a young man" dressed in "a white robe," but to their amazement they did not see the body of Jesus. Instead they heard the angel proclaiming the resurrection: "He has risen [ἠγέρθη], he is not here." In trembling and astonishment they fled from the tomb, "and they said nothing to any one, for they were afraid" (Mk 16:3-8). The number of angels differs in the narratives. Matthew and Mark mention one, and two appear in Luke and John. All agree, however, that the angel or angels came as heavenly messengers, witnesses and interpreters of the resurrection.

The basic agreement among the evangelists in their accounts of what happened on the first Easter morning is more significant than certain discrepancies in those accounts. All four evangelists bear witness to the empty tomb, either stating this explicitly or, like St Mark, clearly implying it.[1] The variations in the accounts actually testify to their authenticity and serve as an important

---

[1]See Vincent Taylor, *The Gospel according to St. Mark* (London: Macmillan, 1959) 606.

indicator that the story of the empty tomb belongs to the most primitive gospel tradition. It is highly unlikely that the empty tomb stories could be legendary embellishments of a later period in the life of the Church, for if the Church had fabricated them, we should expect the Christian community to have created a harmonious account. The Church did not try to harmonize the accounts, but instead faithfully transmitted the traditions that were received.

The lack of uniformity also attests to the historical character of the accounts in describing the reaction of the women who discovered the empty tomb "on the third day." It was revealed to them that the empty tomb was the consequence of the resurrection of Christ. The evangelist Mark, by stressing the fear or awe of the women, tells us that the empty tomb was the primary visible sign of the resurrection. Their fear is a genuine example of an experience of what Rudolf Otto has characterized as the *mysterium tremendum*.[2] They responded to this unexpected, transcendent event of life having emerged from the tomb with awe and silence—a silence more expressive than words. St Luke describes the women as perplexed and frightened. They bowed their faces to the ground when they saw the "two men," that is, the two angels, standing by them. "Why do you seek the living among the dead?" the angels asked them (Lk 24:5). In the Gospel of St Matthew the women undergo a similar experience. Mary Magdalene and the "other Mary" departed from the tomb "with fear and great joy" (Mt 28:8), for, writes St John Chrysostom, "they had seen a thing amazing, and beyond expectation, a tomb empty, where they had before seen [Jesus] laid."[3] Whether the message of the resurrection is delivered by "an angel," as in Matthew, or by "two men," as

[2]The term *mysterium* indicates the supernatural, transcendent character of the Holy One. He is the "wholly other" and there is nothing that can be compared with him. The adjective *tremendum* points to the awe experienced when one encounters the "wholly other." On the *mysterium tremendum*, as well as the "numinous sense," see Rudolf Otto, *The Idea of the Holy* (London: Oxford University Press, 1923) 1-40.

[3]*Homilies on Matthew* 89, in Philip Schaff, ed., *A Select Library of the Nicene and Post-Nicene Fathers of the Christian Church*, 1st series [NPNF], 14 vols. (New York, 1887-1894) 10:527.

in Luke, the message is authoritative and clear: the event of the resurrection had occurred.

Mary Magdalene and the other women with her are mentioned in all four resurrection accounts as the first witnesses to the empty tomb.[4] St John mentions only Mary Magdalene, but this does not exclude the possibility that some other women were with her on that eventful morning (see John 20:2—"*We* do not know where they have laid him"). She was also the first to see the risen Christ (Jn 20:11-18; Mk 16:9). It is most improbable that the narratives about the women and the empty tomb were created later in order to satisfy some need of the Church. What benefit could the Church have had from them? The gospels were written in a world and in an atmosphere that distrusted the witness of women. Nevertheless, the evangelists, drawing on the tradition of the Church, recorded their names and their witness. These women had followed Jesus from Galilee to Jerusalem; they served him, saw him crucified and buried, and witnessed to the discovery of the empty tomb. Their names and work are not the product of the creative imagination of the gospel writers but belong to the remembered and relived past. By attributing to the women—rather than to Peter, James or John—such an important and significant role on the first Easter Sunday, the evangelists must have followed with complete faithfulness the facts transmitted to the Church of the earliest times.

With the words "He is risen" the angel in Mark refers to the resurrection as something that has already happened. The moment of the resurrection itself, however, is not narrated. No human being was a witness to the very moment when Jesus rose from the tomb. The angel appears already as a heavenly witness to the resurrection before the human witnesses found the tomb empty and saw the risen Christ. St Matthew affirms that the women were the first to find the tomb empty as well as the first to meet and worship Christ after the resurrection (28:1-10), yet he does not say that this moment or even this day of the discovery and appearance is the very point when the

---

[4]On why neither Mary Magdalene nor the other women are mentioned by St Paul in 1 Cor 15:3ff, see below, 87-8.

resurrection took place. The angel, according to Matthew, descended from heaven and rolled back the stone not to facilitate the resurrection, not to aid the Messiah who suffered on the cross and was buried, but to enable the women to see that the tomb was empty and that Christ was already risen from the dead (28:2ff). The angel took away the stone, in the words of St John Chrysostom, "that [the women] might believe that He was risen, [that] they see the sepulchre void of the body. For this cause he removed the stone, for this cause also an earthquake took place, that they might be thoroughly aroused and awakened."[5]

The iconography of the resurrection in the Orthodox Church also does not present the very moment when Christ was raised from the dead. The scriptures did not admit any depiction of this moment, and therefore it was not portrayed in early Christian art.[6] Icons depicting the moment of the resurrection were created only in a much later period by iconographers who were influenced by the art of the Renaissance.[7] The ancient tradition of Orthodox iconography actually contains two icons of the resurrection: the icon of the descent of Christ into Hades and the icon portraying the myrrhbearing women at the sepulcher. The first is a "theological" witness to the resurrection, depicting an event that was not seen and that could not have been seen by any human being, although it is referred to in the New Testament (Mt 27:52f; Acts 2:27, 31; Eph 4:8-10; 1 Pet 3:19-4:6). This icon is linked with the

[5] *Homilies on Matthew* 89, NPNF 10:527.

[6] There were efforts to narrate the moment of the resurrection in the apocryphal *Gospel of Peter* and the *Gospel of the Hebrews,* which the Church did not accept. See Edgar Hennecke, *New Testament Apocrypha,* 2 vols. (Philadelphia: Westminster Press, 1963) 1:185-6; and below, 89 and n.

[7] Gustaf Aulen writes that until the thirteenth century the crucified Christ was depicted as a martyr, but a martyr who in martyrdom is victorious. "In the later Middle Ages a change set in. People now enjoyed depicting suffering in all its cruelty and horror." When the New Testament speaks of believers sharing in the sufferings of Christ, "it speaks at the same time of sharing in 'the power of his resurrection' and in his 'glory.' " Gustaf Aulen, *Drama and the Symbols* (Philadelphia: Fortress Press, 1970) 168, 171. When the resurrection is viewed separately from the cross, it can then be portrayed in a spiritualized manner. However, the cross and the resurrection must be viewed together in order to avoid distorting the image of Christ in the New Testament.

services of Holy Saturday, which express the purpose and result of Christ's descent into Hades. The second icon is a "historical" one, based on what happened on the first day of the week as recorded in the gospels, and is of particular importance for an understanding of the link between the cross, the tomb and the resurrection.[8]

The resurrection is an act of God, and the message of the resurrection must first of all come from him. His angel or messenger tells the women not to be afraid, and then informs them of the resurrection. In St John's gospel the two angels do not proclaim it, however. Instead, Jesus in his risen body greets Mary Magdalene outside the tomb and gives her the message for the apostles (Jn 20:11-18).

The Tomb in the Gospel of St John

After Mary Magdalene saw the stone moved away from the tomb and ran to inform Peter and the other disciple that "They have taken the Lord out of the tomb, and we do not know where they have laid him" (Jn 20:2), the two disciples themselves ran to the tomb. The beloved disciple, who is usually identified as John, reached the tomb first and looked in and "saw the linen cloths lying there" and also "the napkin [τὸ σουδάριον] which had been on his head, not lying with the linen cloths but rolled up in a place by itself" (20:4-7). On account of what he had just seen, the beloved disciple "believed" (ἐπίστευσεν, 20:8). This is the only instance we have of someone believing in the resurrection of Christ solely due to the discovery of the empty tomb. All the other followers of Christ, including Peter, came to believe only after the risen Christ appeared to them.

John did not believe in the resurrection simply because the tomb was empty. As a matter of fact, it was not "empty." The beloved disciple believed because he noticed the arrangement of the linen cloths and the napkin, and he took this to be a sign or evidence of the resurrection. If the body had been stolen,

---

[8]On these icons see Leonid Ouspensky and Vladimir Lossky, *The Meaning of Icons* (Boston, 1952) 189-92. See plates 3 and 4.

those who took it would not have troubled to leave the linen
cloths and the napkin undisturbed, in their proper places.
Peter, who also saw the arrangement of the burial cloths,
returned home "amazed at what had happened" (Lk 24:12
JB), but without seeing the position of these articles as a sign
of the resurrection. For the beloved disciple, however, what he
saw in the tomb was clear evidence that the body of Jesus had
not been stolen or removed by human hands, as Mary Magdalene had feared, but that Jesus was risen.

The position of the napkin is a very important detail in the
Gospel of St John. He records it to indicate that Christ, having
risen from the dead, will not die again, and this is what essentially distinguishes Christ's resurrection from the resurrection
of Lazarus. Lazarus came out of the tomb with "his hands and
feet bound with bandages, and his face wrapped with a cloth
[σουδαρίῳ]" (Jn 11:44). Jesus was raised with the soudarion
left in the tomb, while Lazarus emerged with the soudarion
still on him. The same word is used by the evangelist in both
accounts, and provides a basis for comparison between the two
resurrections. The burial napkin is a sign of death, and the fact
that Lazarus still bears it means that he will die again and wait
for the general resurrection. When the burial napkin is left in
the tomb of Christ, however, it becomes a sign of life and
resurrection, after which there will be no more death.[9] Jesus
was raised to glory, and his is the resurrection of the age to
come. Death no longer has any power over him. He has offered
himself only once (see Hb 9:25-28).

Although the beloved disciple believed in the resurrection
of Christ upon seeing the empty but orderly tomb, he did not
say anything to anybody about it until he had himself seen the
risen Christ.[10] Although he believed, even in his case seeing the
tomb was not by itself a compelling reason for the proclamation of the resurrection. His silence seems not to have been

[9]See a very informative article by William E. Reiser, "The Case of the
Tidy Tomb: The Place of the Napkins of John 11:44 and 20:7," *Heythrop
Journal* 14:1 (1973) 47-57. Here Jn 5:19-29 is seen as a commentary on the
rising of Lazarus, and Jn 10:17-18 on the rising of Jesus. The napkin appears
as a sign of glory.

[10]There is an interesting discussion on this point in Gustav Stählin, "On
the Third Day," *Interpretation* 10:3 (1956) 286.

caused by fear but by faith that was not yet "complete." Only after Jesus appeared to him and the other disciples and they had received the Holy Spirit would the beloved disciple possess the fulness of faith (Jn 20:19-23).

St Paul and the Empty Tomb

There is no explicit reference to the empty tomb in the writings of St Paul. This has led some scholars to assume that he was ignorant of it. If St Paul had known of the empty tomb, their argument runs, he undoubtedly would have mentioned it. On this basis they conclude that the story of the women coming on the first day of the week and finding the tomb of Jesus empty must be of a later origin.

When taken in context, however, several passages in the epistles of the apostle Paul do imply his knowledge of the empty tomb. In the letter to the Romans, for instance, where the meaning of baptism is expounded, Paul suggests that the tomb was empty: "when we were baptised we went into the tomb with him and joined him in death, so that as Christ was raised from the dead by the Father's glory, we too might live a new life" (Rm 6:4 JB).[11] If entering the tomb here means to die, then by the structure of this sentence to rise (ἐγείρειν) means to leave the tomb. This connection of baptism with death and resurrection is characteristic of Paul's thought. He also implies knowledge of the empty tomb in 1 Corinthians 15:42ff, when he uses the expressions "physical" and "spiritual" body and compares the resurrection to a seed that is sown or buried in the ground and rises in another form. In the letter to the Philippians he speaks about the transformation of the same body that entered the tomb, not about replacing the body in the tomb with a new body in the resurrection (Ph 3:21). If St Paul did not know of the empty tomb and did not think it important for faith, then we would have to assume that he

[11]The expression "we went into the tomb with him" (συνετάφημεν) is rendered "we were buried with him" in the RSV. The verb used here is a compound of σὺν (with) and θάπτεσθαι (to be buried, to be placed in a sepulcher), which derives from τάφος (tomb, sepulcher). Thus the Jerusalem Bible rendition.

conceived of the resurrection as a kind of spiritual awakening not involving the body—an idea that is foreign to the whole course of his thought.[12]

The very expression that Jesus was "raised up" implies that the tomb in which he was buried was empty at the resurrection. Both the noun "resurrection" (ἀνάστασις) and the verb "to rise, to raise up" (ἐγείρειν) include by themselves a "movement of the body"—the body did not remain in the tomb.[13] These words are used to point to the bodily character of the resurrection. It is not simply a spiritual awakening of the soul, but the resurrection of soul and body.

The empty tomb is also implied in the preaching ascribed to St Paul in the book of Acts, when Paul states that "he whom God raised up saw no corruption" (13:37). The body did not remain in the tomb and decompose, but was raised. Paul's statement of the kerygma of the Church, which he received and faithfully transmitted to the communities he taught, likewise implies that the tomb was found empty and the body of Jesus transformed. In 1 Corinthians 15:4-5 we have the following sequence of events: burial, resurrection, appearances—not burial followed immediately by appearances, which would suggest that the empty tomb is not important. For St Paul the empty tomb is of great importance—it is inseparable from the resurrection. Those among modern scholars who see in St Paul's omission of a direct reference to the empty tomb any proof that the doctrine of the bodily resurrection is of later origin are simply in conflict with the witness of the New Testament.

It is true that after his conversion Paul does not go to verify whether the tomb is empty. However, this was not a primary question for him. Before his conversion, while he was persecuting the Christians in Jerusalem, he doubtless heard more than once about the Christian claims about the empty tomb and the appearances of their crucified leader. He knew that the tomb was empty, and he also knew that nobody had been able to produce the corpse and thereby repudiate and destroy once and for all the claims of the disciples of Jesus. Paul further-

---

[12]See below, chapter 7, "The Bodily Resurrection."

[13]Jindrich Mánek, "The Apostle Paul and the Empty Tomb," *Novum Testamentum* 2 (1958) 276-7.

more was aware before his conversion that the fact of the empty tomb itself was not enough to prove that the resurrection had occurred. Both the disciples and their opponents agreed that the tomb was empty, but disagreed radically as to why. The disciples believed that it was empty because Jesus had risen from the dead. Their opponents, on the other hand, insisted that the body had been stolen, and it was for this reason that the tomb had been found empty (cf Mt 28:11-15). Only when Christ appeared to him on the road to Damascus was Paul certain that Jesus had risen from the dead, and that this was the true reason why the tomb was empty.[14]

Some Modern Interpreters and the Empty Tomb

Generally speaking, there is a tendency in modern scholarship to minimize the importance of the empty tomb or to avoid ascribing too much significance to it. One of the best known treatments of this subject, Kirsopp Lake's *The Historical Evidence for the Resurrection of Jesus Christ* (1907), rejects the evidence of the empty tomb as recorded in the gospels. A modern reviewer, A.M. Ramsey, has pointed out how Lake refuses to accept the resurrection, for he believes in "the unbroken survival of personal life," which denies and excludes the reality of bodily resurrection as presented in the New Testament. What he has to say about the resurrection of Christ is not based upon the historical fact he investigates, however, but upon his clearly spelled out assumptions. He writes, for instance, that "the story of the empty tomb must be fought out on doctrinal, not on historical or critical grounds."[15]

Another, more modern, exegete, John A. T. Robinson, concedes that Paul knew about the empty tomb, but that the resurrection of Jesus might still be true even if his bones "*could* yet be lying around Palestine." The empty tomb has no importance in his theological understanding of the resurrection of Christ.

[14]See the valuable discussion in Michael Dummett, "Biblical Exegesis and the Resurrection," *New Blackfriars* 58:681 (1977) 56-72.

[15]See A. M. Ramsey, *The Resurrection of Christ* (New York: Fontana Books, 1961) 52f.

He rejects the assumption that faith in the resurrection was born on the basis of "people's tall stories" and instead prefers to ground faith in "a corporate spiritual awareness of Christ no longer as a dead memory, however vivid, but as a vivifying presence."[16] But what or who brought about this "spiritual awareness" or "vivifying presence"? The same author has elsewhere recognized that the data on the empty tomb is too strongly rooted in the New Testament tradition to be dismissed as a creation of a legendary character,[17] and yet he discards the story of the empty tomb on his theological grounds.

Even those who have made significant contributions to our understanding of the historical and theological aspects of the resurrection and the message of Easter have displayed ambiguities in their interpretation of the empty tomb. They recognize that the tomb was empty not because biblical anthropology presupposed that the body should no longer be in the tomb but because the women found it empty, yet they avoid concluding from our primary sources that the disciples themselves actually bore witness to the discovery of the empty tomb. They avoid this conclusion because of the "silence" of St Paul as well as the fact that all other authors of the New Testament except the evangelists "ignored" it. Here again, if the fact of the empty tomb is not rejected outright, it is neither asserted nor presented as essential for a proper understanding of the resurrection of Christ.

Those modern interpreters who minimize the importance of the empty tomb, basing their conclusion on the "silence" or

[16]John A. T. Robinson, *Can We Trust the New Testament?* (Grand Rapids, Mich.: Eerdmans, 1977) 124, 126.

[17]See Robinson's article "Resurrection in the NT," in G. A. Buttrick, ed., *Interpreter's Dictionary of the Bible*, 4 vols. (New York: Abingdon Press, 1962) 4:43-53. Peter Selby has analyzed Robinson's position quite succinctly. He writes that "as a historian of the New Testament [Robinson] is convinced that the evidence cannot be made to square with the possibility that the bones of Jesus may be around in Palestine; as an apologist anxious to commend Christian faith he wishes to be free (or his hearers to be free) to believe that they are." He concludes that "it is hardly likely that such a position as he advocates will succeed in doing justice either to the earliest Christian apologetic . . . or to the needs of contemporary apologetic in a world which continues to ask what took place." Peter Selby, *Look for the Living: The Contemporary Nature of Resurrection Faith* (Philadelphia: Fortress Press, 1976) 56.

"disregard" of the New Testament writers, experience difficulties in dealing with the evidence the New Testament terminology offers us. Two fundamental terminologies for interpreting the new life of Christ were at the disposal of the New
Testament authors: the terminology of resurrection and the
terminology of exaltation or glorification. What happened in
the New Testament is quite clear: the terminology of resurrection triumphed over and absorbed the terminology of exaltation, and precisely because of the fact that "exaltation" was
less adequate a term for embracing and expressing the evidence
of the resurrection. In particular, "exaltation" did not necessarily imply the empty tomb, which was always taken for
granted whenever the authors of the New Testament employed
the terminology of resurrection. It is true that for them as well
as for us the Easter faith is faith in the risen Lord and not
faith in the empty tomb, but it is also true that the Church of
the New Testament—and the Church throughout the centuries
as well, for that matter—could not fully have believed in and
developed the doctrine of the living Christ without at the same
time believing and asserting that his tomb was found empty.
The preaching of the resurrection originated in Jerusalem, and
the community of the resurrected Christ in the holy city came
into existence due first of all to the well-attested fact that the
empty tomb was located there. Faith in the resurrection as the
New Testament knows and professes it would have been forever refuted if the body of Jesus had been discovered.

As we have seen, the empty tomb by itself did not produce
this faith or compel the disciples to believe in the resurrection.
Only all the facts taken together—the empty tomb, the post-
resurrection appearances and the Church born and guided by
the Spirit—can serve as the foundation for faith in the resurrection. In the Orthodox Church the altar in a certain sense represents the sepulcher, and the climax of the Sunday Vigil service
coincides with the reading of the gospel of the resurrection
from that altar. The resurrection is proclaimed again from the
holy sepulcher, the tomb becomes anew the source of life.

On the Third Day

The gospels are historical and theological documents. Their theology cannot be divorced from the historical events they record. But before we start collecting data and references as to where and how the expression "the third day" is used and what meaning is ascribed to it in biblical thought, we must remember that the event in the New Testament that took place "on the third day" belongs to history. The cluster of events of the passion week has a definite chronological framework. This "third day" appears in the earliest gospel texts not to convey a "temporary residence"[18] of Jesus in the tomb or to demonstrate that the soul abides in the body for three days after death, but because it was on the third day that the tomb was found empty. The charge by the Jewish authorities that the disciples of Jesus stole his body presupposes that the events actually occurred in the sequence given in the New Testament. No contemporaries ever made a counter claim that the body was still in the tomb, that nothing actually happened "on the third day."[19]

The expressions "on the third day" and "after three days" appear repeatedly in the Old Testament. The first and probably most obvious passage that comes to mind is Hosea 6:2: "After two days he will revive us; on the third day he will raise us up, that we may live before him." Although it was never quoted in the New Testament books, this verse influenced many rabbinical writers, who believed that the resurrection of the dead would follow the end of the world, and that it would occur on

[18]The phrase "three days" is found in ancient Near Eastern religious traditions in reference to a "temporary habitation"—the "fourth day" implies a "permanent residence." On this basis it has been speculated that with the expression "on the third day" the Church wanted to convey the idea that Jesus "was only a temporary visitor in the house of the dead." See H. Anderson, *Jesus and Christian Origins* (New York: Oxford University Press, 1964) 214.

[19]Arthur Darby Nock asserts that in the gospels "this *third* day rests on an elaborate chronological framework of circumstances which we must regard either as historical or as a complete fabrication." Our primary sources are very clear and definite on this point without variations, and "the simple explanation of the tradition which the first Christians bequeathed is that it represents their impression of what had happened." See his *Early Gentile Christianity and its Hellenistic Background* (New York: Harper Torchbooks, 1964) 108.

the third day thereafter. It has been suggested that Jesus had this verse from Hosea in mind in the three passion prophecies (Mk 8:31, 9:31, 10:33-34). Hosea speaks in this verse about the restoration of Israel; Jesus points out that the coming of the new people of God will spring from his death and resurrection (Jn 12:20ff).

We also find the expression "on the third day" in the story of the sacrifice of Isaac (Gn 22). God provided a substitute sacrifice on the "third day" (22:4) after he ordered Abraham to sacrifice his son. This is the day of deliverance, of the unbinding of Isaac. We meet the phrase "three days" in the book of Joshua: "At the end of three days," after Joshua and his people reached the Jordan River, "the officers went through the camp and commanded the people, 'When you see the ark of the covenant of the Lord your God being carried by the Levitical priests, then you shall set out from your place and follow it' " (3:2-3). And on that day, after three days on the banks, the people of Israel crossed the river into the promised land. Other references to three days are found, for example, in Jonah 1:17 (2:1 in the Hebrew Bible) and in 2 Kings 20:5.

Thus, the event of the discovery of the empty tomb prompted the disciples to search the scriptures, to see in them the light of the resurrection and to learn, as Chrysostom puts it, that not "at random were these things done."[20] There is an inner connection between the events of the two covenants, for they belong to the divine plan of salvation.

The designated readings from the Old Testament for Holy Saturday illustrate this inner connection. There are fifteen such readings, the first of which is taken from the creation story of the beginning of Genesis. Let us review this account in the context of our discussion of the origin of the "third day" tradition. What should be mentioned first of all is that only the section dealing with the first three days of creation (Gn 1:1-13) is read. The reading significantly stops with the third day of creation, on which God commands the earth to produce its own fruits, the first fruits of the first creation. And on this day the earth responded and "brought forth vegetation, plants yielding

---

[20]*Homilies on Matthew* 38, NPNF 10:228.

seed according to their own kinds, and trees bearing fruit in which is their seed, each according to its kind. And God saw that it was good. And there was evening and there was morning, a third day" (1:12-13). As in the other readings for Holy Saturday, we have here an indication of how the Church interpreted scripture in the light of the resurrection. The historical fact of the finding of the empty tomb influenced the selection of texts from the Old Testament to be read at the service commemorating the victory of Christ over death. Like seed bearing fruit on the third day, the body of Christ, this unique seed, dies to bear much fruit (Jn 12:24). He is the "first fruits of those who have fallen asleep" (1 Cor 15:20). The creative power of God was manifested on the third day of creation, and with the resurrection of Christ on the third day the new creation began. Thus the meaning of Genesis 1:1-13 is brought out for the Church.

Some of the Old Testament passages read on Holy Saturday in the Orthodox Church also remind the faithful that Jesus embodies the true Israel, that the resurrection is true deliverance and that through the death and resurrection of Christ we enter the "promised land."

The Church makes this appeal to the scriptures to show the unity between the old and the new covenants, to proclaim the resurrection and to strengthen our understanding of it. St John Chrysostom wrote that the fact of the death of Christ was known to all, "but that he suffered this for the sins of the world" was not. Therefore, "the testimony from the scriptures" is brought in.[21] The empty tomb was seen by witnesses, but the scriptures were brought in to corroborate the fact of the resurrection of Christ itself, which did not have human witnesses.

The empty tomb as a historical fact by itself is subject to various interpretations, but only within its larger context can its meaning and importance be revealed. The empty tomb is the sign of the resurrection and the evidence of the incarnation. It points to the resurrection, and at the same time affirms that the body of the incarnate Son of God, although mortal, could not be subject to corruption but underwent transfiguration and

[21]Ibid., 229.

glorification. The stone rolled back from the tomb signifies that Jesus is no longer separated from the living, and the angel sitting on that stone in front of the empty tomb is the sign of the victory of life over death. The disciples and apostles to whom the risen Christ appeared and who recognized him have witnessed to his resurrection by their lives and deaths—they have become living proofs of it.

5

"He Appeared unto Many"

After his resurrection from the dead, Christ "appeared to Cephas, then to the twelve. Then he appeared to more than five hundred brethren at one time, most of whom are still alive, though some have fallen asleep. Then he appeared to James, then to all the apostles. Last of all, as to one untimely born, he appeared also to me," wrote St Paul in 1 Corinthians 15:5-8. Those mentioned here received a privileged experience from the Lord: the actual, physical appearance of the risen Christ. When they saw the risen Christ, they recognized him to be the same Jesus of Nazareth that they (with the exception of Paul) followed before his crucifixion, and they all believed. Thus, they were able to affirm the testimony of the women who discovered the empty tomb and received their apostolic mission to go and proclaim the resurrection of Christ from the dead.

One striking fact about St Paul's list of those to whom the risen Christ appeared is the absence of the women. All four gospels specifically mention Mary Magdalene as the first, along with the women with her, to discover the empty tomb and meet the risen Christ, yet her name and the names of the other women are not included in the primitive kerygma, the most complete list of witnesses we have to the post-resurrection appearances of Christ.

The most probable reason why they were omitted from the kerygma was that it was written in the form of an official document, an official recital of the central events in the life of Christ, and thus would require official witnesses. At the time it was written, such witnesses had to be men, not women. The composition of the kerygma corresponded to the legal demands of the time, which excluded women from being legally accepted witnesses.[1] We may presume then that these names were left out not because the risen Christ did not appear to them and not because St Paul did not know of their visit to the tomb on the first Easter, but because the primitive Church selected from among the witnesses only those whose qualifications could not be questioned from a legal point of view. By not mentioning the women the kerygma in no way whatsoever casts any shadow of doubt over their witness, nor does it minimize the authenticity and truthfulness of the gospel accounts, which give the women a very prominent role in the events of the first Easter Sunday.

The "Official" Witnesses to the Resurrection

St Paul's account lists two proper names—Peter (Cephas) and James—and then Paul adds his own. Peter, as the spokesman of the disciples, was the first to confess Jesus to be the Messiah or the Christ (Mk 8:27-30), and Peter was the first among them to appear as an official witness to the resurrection. The credal statement "he appeared to Cephas" (1 Cor 15:5) is supported by the Gospel of St Luke, who in his "Gospel of the Resurrection" records the events of the "first day of the week" (24:1). Two disciples, after having seen Christ on the road to Emmaus, returned to Jerusalem to be told by the eleven and those with them that "The Lord has risen indeed, and has appeared [ὤφθη] to Simon!" (24:34) The leadership role

[1]In Judaism a woman was not qualified to give testimony, "because it was concluded from Gen. 18:15 that she was a liar." Only in a few exceptional cases was her witness accepted, and in the same cases where a gentile slave's testimony was acceptable. His study of this topic gives Joachim Jeremias the impression that "Judaism in Jesus' time also had a very low opinion of women, which is usual in the Orient where she is chiefly valued for her fecundity, kept as far as possible shut away from the outer world, submissive to the power of her father or her husband, and where she is inferior to men from a religious point of view." See his *Jerusalem in the Time of Jesus: An Investigation into Economic and Social Conditions during the New Testament Period* (Philadelphia: Fortress Press, 1969) 374-6. Against this background we can appreciate the very different attitude toward women that Jesus showed.

that Simon Peter played in the earliest Christian community in Jerusalem would be beyond intelligible explanation unless Jesus had appeared to him. Peter had denied Christ, but the appearance to him signified the end of his despairing condition, according to some patristic writers. Christ appeared to Peter to comfort him. Both ancient and modern interpreters point out that Peter's authority in the early Church was not the result of his own strength and singlemindedness, but was derived from his meeting with the risen Christ.

James, who came after Peter as the head of the Church in Jerusalem (Acts 12:17, 15:13ff, 21:18ff; Ga 1:18ff, 2:9 and 12) likewise did not acquire his position by the strength of his personality, but because Christ had also appeared to him. This James had not even been a member of the twelve. He is known to us as the "brother of the Lord," and during the public ministry of Jesus his "brothers" (or cousins) had not even believed in him (Jn 7:5). Outside of the evidence of the kerygma in 1 Corinthians 15:7 we have no corroboration of the appearance of Christ to James. However, the *Gospel of the Hebrews*, one of the apocryphal gospels of the second century that was not created under gnostic influence, contains a rather detailed account of the circumstances under which Christ came to James after his resurrection:

> And when the Lord had given the linen cloth to the servant of the priest, he went to James and appeared to him. For James had sworn that he would not eat bread from that hour in which he had drunk the cup of the Lord until he should see him risen from among them that sleep. And shortly thereafter the Lord said: Bring a table and bread! And immediately it was added: he took the bread, blessed it and brake it and gave it to James the Just and said to him: My brother, eat thy bread, for the Son of Man is risen from among them that sleep.[2]

[2] See Edgar Hennecke, *New Testament Apocrypha,* 2 vols. (Philadelphia: Westminster Press, 1963) 1:165. According to this apocryphal gospel, the resurrection was seen by those guarding the tomb, when the risen Christ gave the linen cloth to the priest's servant. But in none of the canonical gospels is

The third person mentioned in the kerygmatic summary is Paul. Christ appeared to him "last of all," and because the case of Paul is different from the others we shall discuss the nature, characteristics and meaning of this revelation in the next chapter.

After the appearance to Peter, Christ manifested himself to the eleven, as the gospels amply attest (Lk 24:36-53; Jn 20:19-23; Mt 28:16-20). Then he appeared to "more than five hundred brethren" (1 Cor 15:6), for which we do not have any other reference. Some interpreters have thought that this appearance is represented in Acts 2, the story of Pentecost, but this suggestion is purely speculative. The only common element between the post-resurrection appearance to the five hundred and Pentecost is the large number of people involved in both cases. No account of the post-resurrection appearances, moreover, suggests that the witnesses had charismatic experiences resembling those that accompanied the descent of the Holy Spirit at Pentecost. Hence, we must assume that 1 Corinthians 15:6 and Acts 2 are not two different accounts of the same event but refer to two different occurrences in the post-resurrection period.

The role of Peter and of the others to whom Christ appeared and who became the official apostolic witnesses to the resurrection is unique. Nobody can replace them in this privileged role. They were entrusted with the apostolic mission, and all who have accepted and believed in their testimony share in the same faith with them.

---

the moment of the resurrection itself seen. Therefore, what we find here is not a further development of the other accounts, but a free creation based on the credal statement transmitted in 1 Cor 15:7. The *Gospel of the Hebrews* contradicts the tradition contained in the New Testament on other important points as well. It came from Jewish Christian circles, whose character it reflects, and contains a strong apologetic element. It is worth noting that the gnostic *Gospel of Thomas* also exalts James, and likewise by applying canonical passages in different contexts. See Robert M. Grant, *The Secret Sayings of Jesus: The Gnostic Gospel of Thomas* (Garden City, N.Y.: Doubleday, 1960) 19-37, 128. A clear account of the position of James in early Christianity is given in F. F. Bruce, *Peter, Stephen, James, and John: Studies in Early Non-Pauline Christianity* (Grand Rapids, Mich.: Eerdmans, 1979) 86-119.

The Location and Chronology of the Appearances

There are many other references to appearances of Christ in the New Testament besides those in the "official" list of St Paul. Taken all together, the various appearances of the risen Christ for a long time have raised difficulties for scholars who attempt to harmonize the accounts and establish a definite chronological order for them as well as exactly where they occurred.

Where did Christ appear? In Galilee, in Jerusalem or in both locations? Various answers have been offered to this question. The evangelists are indeed not unanimous in their records. According to three gospel accounts, the risen Christ appeared to the women on the first day of the week in Jerusalem (Mt 28:9-10; Mk 16:9; Jn 20:11-18), and then to the eleven (Mk 16:14ff; Lk 24:33ff; Jn 20:19ff). However, the Gospel of Matthew records only one appearance to the eleven in Galilee, the Gospel of Luke records only appearances in Jerusalem and John mentions appearances to the eleven in Jerusalem as well as to the seven disciples in Galilee (Mt 28:16ff; Lk 24:33ff; Jn 20:19ff and 21:1ff). Where did Christ actually first appear to the eleven?

Even those who are most convinced of the trustworthiness of the gospels as records of the events that preceded and followed the death of Christ show varying degrees of uncertainty about the chronology and location of the appearances. They try to arrange these post-resurrection appearances in order, but can only tentatively identify their location. This comes from diversities in the gospel records, and it is understandable that there should be indecisiveness among the interpreters. The number, order and circumstances of the appearances are open to question. We should always bear in mind, however, that these discrepancies "stem from the variety of the testimonies which the evangelists incorporated in their respective gospels without attempting to harmonize differences," as Georges Barrois has observed.[3]

[3]Georges Barrois, *Scripture Readings in Orthodox Worship* (Crestwood, N.Y.: SVS Press, 1977) 104.

Some interpreters are inclined to accept the historical priority of Galilee. When the tomb was found empty the disciples were still in Jerusalem, but in hiding. They were frightened and bewildered, and decided to move to Galilee in the hope that the resurrected Christ would meet them there (Mk 16:7; Mt 28:10). One adherent of this line of interpretation argues that it was in Galilee that the first disciples of Jesus were called, taught by him and incorporated into the messianic community. From there they were sent to proclaim the coming of the kingdom of God. They followed Jesus to Jerusalem, but after his death, already knowing about the empty tomb, they left Jerusalem for Galilee. And there, in the Galilean atmosphere, the risen Christ "wanted to renew in them the decision of the first meeting" and to "complete his revelation."[4] After reaching Galilee, their home, they were given the privilege of seeing the Lord, and with the appearance of their master they finally understood why the tomb was found empty.

This is a quite plausible reconstruction of the movement of the disciples. However, the gospels also say that Jesus appeared in Jerusalem. It would have been normal for the disciples, who were Galileans, to return to their homes from Jerusalem after the Passover celebration. And as pious Jews they might be expected, as C.F.D. Moule argues, to go back to Jerusalem later, for the Feast of Weeks (Pentecost). During the Passover they had seen Christ in Jerusalem, and he appeared again to them upon their return to Galilee. Christ's prediction given after the Last Supper—"I will go before [προάξω] you to Galilee" (Mk 14:28)—as well as the words of the "young man" at the tomb who told the women to tell the apostles that the risen Jesus "is going before you [προάγει ὑμᾶς] to Galilee" (Mk 16:7) need only mean, in Moule's view, that "when you return to Galilee (as you naturally will) you will find that He has preceded you."[5]

In both lines of interpretation that we have outlined regarding the movements of the disciples after the resurrection, there

---

[4] A Monk of the Eastern Church, *Jesus: A Dialogue with the Saviour* (New York: Desclee, 1963) 174.

[5] C. F. D. Moule, "The Post-Resurrection Appearances in the Light of Festival Pilgrimages," *New Testament Studies* 4 (1957-1958) 58-61.

is agreement that the disciples knew of the empty tomb before they moved from Jerusalem to Galilee, but they differ as to "where" and "when" Christ appeared to his disciples. A third attempt to reconstruct the events after the crucifixion has it that the eleven found out about the empty tomb only later. Those who propose this hypothesis speculate that the disciples heard the story of the women about the empty tomb only after they came back to Jerusalem from Galilee to celebrate the concluding feast of the Passover season, Pentecost. In Galilee they had experienced a kind of "revelatory encounter" with Jesus, leading them to believe in the resurrection. Later, after their return to Jerusalem, they heard the account of the empty tomb and found that it fit in well with their new faith in the resurrection.[6] This view actually does little justice to the evidence of the gospels. The first two views we outlined showed greater concern for the data of the gospels and took that data more seriously. The major thrust of the gospel witness refutes the hypothesis that the disciples believed in the resurrection of Jesus before they were acquainted with the discovery of the empty tomb. The appearance of Christ to the eleven removed their perplexity as to why it was empty.

We should also mention here another line of interpretation that bases itself on "symbolic geography." When the disciples are told that Christ will precede them to Galilee (Mk 14:28 and 16:7), some interpreters see it as a "theological symbol" or a "symbolic Galilee." Geographical references in general in the Gospel of Mark are seen as heavily symbolic. Galilee is viewed as a symbol of the gentile world, to which Christ will lead his disciples. The mission of the Church lies in the gentile

[6]Reginald H. Fuller, in *The Formation of the Resurrection Narratives* (New York: Macmillan, 1971), conjectures that "when the disciples returned from Galilee to Jerusalem after their visions of the Risen One they received from Mary Magdalene a report that she had visited the tomb and discovered it empty" (56). Ulrich Wilckens developed this point of view also in his essay "The Tradition—History of the Resurrection of Jesus," in C. F. D. Moule, ed., *The Significance of the Message of the Resurrection for Faith in Jesus Christ*, Studies in Biblical Theology, 2d series, 8 (London: SCM Press, 1968) 51-76. Wilckens' thesis is that "It was the appearance of the risen Jesus in Galilee which inspired belief in the resurrection . . . Moving to Jerusalem, the community found in existence the women's story of the discovery of the empty tomb" (73-4).

world, and there the disciples will see Christ.[7] This "symbolic geography" reveals extreme skepticism for the historical references in the gospels, and has not won much support.[8]

A somewhat similar but better-grounded exegetical viewpoint sees certain theological perspectives reflected in the account each evangelist furnishes of the order and place of the appearances. Thus, St Luke, who records appearances only in Jerusalem and the area around it, reflects his interest in the holy city. His gospel begins with events in Jerusalem (1:5ff) and finds its fulfilment in that same city (chapter 24). The Galilean appearances would not fit into the "theological geography" of his gospel, and therefore, for theological rather than historical reasons, Luke simply omits the appearances in Galilee and concentrates on those in Jerusalem. For Matthew, on the other hand, Jerusalem did not have the same preeminence because its leaders took part in the crucifixion of Jesus. Consequently, St Matthew records only that he appeared to the eleven in Galilee, and from Galilee the gospel would be spread throughout the world (28:16-20). Matthew too, according to this theory, follows a theological rather than historical logic.[9]

All these theories have their interesting points, yet none can completely solve the problem while taking all the gospel evidence into account. The most we can say is that the bulk of the evidence leads us to conclude that the disciples did know of the empty tomb before they returned to Galilee, they were most likely still in Jerusalem on the first Easter day, and both the appearances in Jerusalem and those in Galilee can be taken as historical.[10] To cite C.F.D. Moule once more, "the appearances in Jerusalem and Galilee will represent, not different conceptions of the Christian mission, but simply the conception

---

[7]Norman Perrin, *The Resurrection according to Matthew, Mark and Luke* (Philadelphia: Fortress Press, 1977) 26-7.

[8]Vincent Taylor, one of the most thorough exegetes of the Gospel of St Mark, has characterized this symbolic interpretation as "slenderly based." See his *The Gospel according to St. Mark* (London: Macmillan, 1959) on Mk 16:7.

[9]On this theory, see the chapter entitled "Chronological and Theological Order in the Gospels," in my book *The Gospel Image of Christ: The Church and Modern Criticism* (Crestwood, N.Y.: SVS Press, 1972) 53-64.

[10]Hans von Campenhausen, "The Event of Easter and the Empty Tomb," in his *Life in the Church* (Philadelphia: Fortress Press, 1968) 42-89.

of Jesus showing himself wherever his friends happened to be at the time."[11]

While various speculations may arise from the discrepancies in the evidence presented to us, we must above all avoid attempting to harmonize our sources. The evangelists did not try to harmonize all their accounts, and neither did the early Church, even though there were apologetic reasons for doing so. The Church preferred to preserve and transmit diverse testimonies. Any harmonization, in order to be consistent, would inevitably exclude some important elements and would produce out of the divine-human witness that we have a human document, based only on human logic. The complexity of the resurrection experience, only partially understood by the participants, would be reduced to a neatly defined sequence of events in the post-resurrection period that would only hinder us from experiencing all that was happening and participating fully in the joy of the resurrection. The accounts we have of the post-resurrection appearances point to the doubt and fear of the participants—surely an argument that refutes the theory that they were created later. These narratives include the most primitive traditions, which converge despite their differences and confirm the truth of what they report. And primitive Christian preaching would be incomprehensible without the different testimonies that the apostles bear to the many and varied meetings with the risen Christ.[12]

Common Characteristics of the Appearances

The discrepancies in the gospel accounts of the post-resurrection appearances of Christ are interesting, particularly in light of the very fact that there are discrepancies. What is more striking, however, are the common characteristics of these various appearances, and the points in common among the accounts have also drawn much attention from scholars and interpreters. The first common aspect that we notice is the

[11]Moule, "Post-Resurrection Appearances," 59-60.
[12]See also the discussion of the *Diatessaron* and the *euaggelion tetramorphon* in the *Gospel Image of Christ*, 72-5.

initiative and freedom of Christ. He comes suddenly, he is present and he is seen, but he is no longer an inhabitant of the earth. In all these appearances we have the risen Jesus who transcends the limitations of space and time—there are no natural limitations to his movements.

The second common aspect of these appearances is that Jesus is recognized, but only after a moment of doubt. Doubt is explicitly mentioned in Matthew 28:17: "And when they saw him they worshiped him; but some doubted [ἐδίστα-σαν]." Does this imply some of the eleven could not believe what they were seeing? We should note that the evangelist does not use the word "disbelieve" or "refuse to believe" (ἀπιστέω) but rather a word connoting wavering, hesitation, vacillation (διστάζω). St Matthew also used the same term in his account of Jesus walking on the water (14:22-33). When Peter, who was walking on the water too, became afraid because of the strong wind and began to sink, Jesus offered his hand and caught him, saying, "O man of little faith, why did you doubt [ἐδίστασας]?" (14:31) It is clear from the context of this story that Peter's doubt cannot be construed to constitute a denial of faith in a formal sense, but means rather that faith is mixed with doubt. Peter walked on the water to come to Jesus, but he was wavering, vacillating, when confronted with danger.[13]

Any disciple of Jesus might experience this doubt. At the time of the appearance some of the eleven were bewildered, and in this moment of crisis in their lives they displayed hesitation or vacillation. The Jerusalem Bible, in fact, translates the phrase "but some doubted" in Matthew 28:17 as "though some hesitated." One investigator into this verse, after an analysis of the meaning of the word for doubting, suggests that the appearance of Christ in Matthew is presented as an "ecclesiastical" event, pointing to the difficulties and challenges of discipleship. This does not imply that doubt does not historically belong

[13]For an exegesis and additional references, see John P. Meier, *The Vision of Matthew: Christ, Church and Morality in the First Gospel* (New York: Paulist Press, 1979) 99. Meier adds that the word διστάζω refers here to "that personal, existential vacillation in the presence of danger or confusion which can seize even the believing disciple" (n88).

Icon Plates

(St. Vladimir's Orthodox Theological Seminary, Crestwood, New York)

PLATE 1—THE HOLY TRINITY

PLATE 2—THE CRUCIFIXION OF OUR LORD

(St. Vladimir's Orthodox Theological Seminary, Crestwood, New York)

PLATE 3—THE DESCENT OF CHRIST INTO HADES

(Courtesy of the Icon Center at the Wijenburgh Castle, 1054 MX Echteld, The Netherlands)

PLATE 4—THE SPICE-BEARING WOMEN AT THE SEPULCHRE

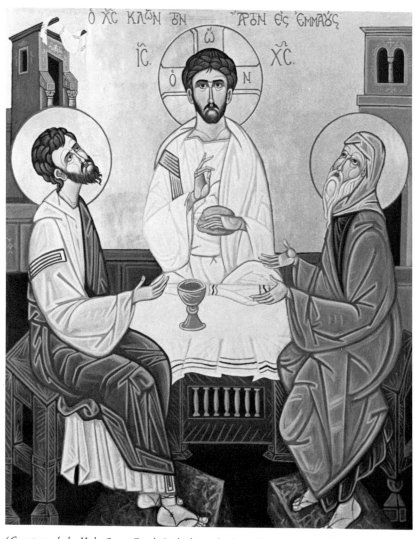

Ο ΧC ΚΛῶΝ ϑΝ ᾺΡϑΝ ΕῙϹ ἘΜΜΑΎϹ

Ι͞C ὼ Χ͞C
Ὀ Ν

(Courtesy of the Holy Cross Greek Orthodox School of Theology, Brookline, Massachusetts)

PLATE 5—CHRIST BREAKING BREAD AT EMMAUS

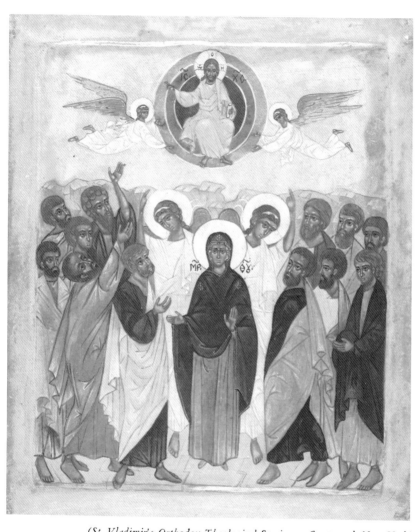

(St. Vladimir's Orthodox Theological Seminary, Crestwood, New York)

PLATE 6—THE ASCENSION OF OUR LORD

PLATE 7—THE DESCENT OF THE HOLY SPIRIT

to the post-resurrection appearances, but rather underlines the point of the whole passage—that the command of the Lord to make disciples of all nations (Mt 28:19) "cannot be done in the strength of man. It is only possible because Christ is with his Church always."[14]

In two other passages that deal with the coming of Christ to his disciples after the resurrection this same doubt is implied. To the women who took hold of his feet and worshiped him Jesus said: "Do not be afraid" or "Fear not" (Mt 28:10). Doubt is also implicit in John 20:19-21. Here Jesus shows the disciples his hands and his side, presumably for two reasons: first, to convince them of the resurrection, and second, to remove their doubt, which had been vocalized by the apostle Thomas.[15]

This experience of doubt belongs to the most primitive tradition of the gospel accounts. The doubt of the disciples may well serve to underline that they were not victims of an illusion and that the appearances did not force faith upon those who witnessed them. Like the empty tomb, the appearances did not automatically bring the disciples to the full conviction that he who had died was raised up, and yet the appearances aroused faith. Everyone to whom Christ appeared believed and became a witness. Doubt prevented recognition, but when it was overcome the disciples experienced gladness and joy, realizing that it was Jesus in their midst. Only after this recognition were they told about their mission. This is a third common characteristic of the appearances. The disciples would not have been sent on their mission if they were not fully convinced that Jesus of Nazareth and the risen Christ are one and the same person. Their mission consists in proclaiming what they have seen and heard.

A final common characteristic of the appearances is that Christ always appeared to friends. Wherever his friends

---

[14]I. P. Ellis, "But Some Doubted," *New Testament Studies* 14:4 (1968) 574-80. P. Benoit has suggested that this doubt or hesitation belongs to the earlier appearances.

[15]A detailed analysis on this point is offered by C. H. Dodd, "The Appearances of the Risen Christ: An Essay in Form-Criticism of the Gospels," in D. E. Nineham, ed., *Studies in the Gospels: Essays in Honor of R. H. Lightfoot* (Oxford: Blackwell, 1955) 10ff.

happened to be, in Jerusalem or in Galilee, Jesus showed himself to them, and not to the High Priest or to Pilate. The only exception was his appearance to Paul while the latter was actively persecuting the Church. The apostle Peter recalls this characteristic of Christ's appearances in his preaching to the household of Cornelius in Caesarea:

> And we are witnesses to all that he did both in the country of the Jews and in Jerusalem. They put him to death by hanging him on a tree; but God raised him up on the third day and made him manifest; not to all the people but to us who were chosen by God as witnesses, who ate and drank with him after he rose from the dead. (Acts 10:39-41)

The renowned Alexandrian theologian and scholar Origen once posed the question "Why did he appear only to friends?" and suggested in answer that not everyone could have endured these encounters with the glorified Christ.[16]

But perhaps we have a more complete answer in Christ's last discourse as presented in John 14:18-21:

> I will not leave you desolate; I will come to you. Yet a little while, and the world will see me no more, but you will see me; because I live, you will live also. . . . He who has my commandments and keeps them, he it is who loves me; and he who loves me will be loved by my

---

[16]The question of Jesus appearing after his resurrection only to friends was raised by the second-century pagan writer Celsus: "If Jesus really wanted to show forth divine power, he ought to have appeared to the very men who treated him despitefully and to the man who condemned him and to everyone everywhere." Origen suggested in answer: "It would not have been right for him to have appeared to the man who condemned him and to those who treated him despitefully. For Jesus had consideration both for the one who condemned him and for those who treated him despitefully, lest they should be smitten with blindness as the men of Sodom were smitten when they conspired in lust for the beauty of the angels lodged at Lot's house . . . Jesus, then, wanted to show forth his divine power to each of those able to see it, and according to the measure of his individual capacity. In fact, perhaps he avoided appearing simply because he was considering the mean abilities of people who had not the capacity to see him." See Henry Chadwick, tr. and ed., *Origen: Contra Celsum* (Cambridge: University Press, 1953) 114ff.

Father, and I will love him and manifest myself to
him.

Jesus speaks of love and of keeping his word as conditions for
being granted his appearance or manifestation. The eastern
fathers interpreted this passage as referring to the resurrection
and post-resurrection appearances. This is the meaning of the
words "yet a little while" and "because I live, you will live
also."

Christ's appearances after his resurrection are neither apocalyptic visions nor revelations of the supernatural world.
Neither can they be considered dreams, for they did not occur
when the disciples were asleep or even at night. When he appears Christ is alone, he unites with himself those who have
been with him, and he speaks to them each time in his own
voice—the voice of the risen Lord, which cannot be mistaken
for any other. The hearts of the disciples burn while he talks
to them (Lk 24:32). What he says is clear, imbued with the
spirit of him who "became a life-giving spirit" (1 Cor 15:45).
The Church kept, treasured, meditated on and transmitted these
words. They belong to its very foundation, for with these words
the disciples were called and sent into the mission to build the
Church (Mt 28:16-20; Jn 20:19-23). They were called to bear
witness to the resurrection among all nations, to baptize, to
forgive and to bring them into the community of the risen
Christ.

These appearances then are the culmination of the miracles
performed in the public ministry of Christ, for the miracles
were also not performed to compel the people to accept Jesus
as the Messiah, but to manifest the power of the kingdom of
God. The post-resurrection appearances are the revelation and
the presence of the risen Christ, who with his coming and
departing reveals himself.

Appearances at Meals

The disciples particularly experienced the joy of reunion
and intimacy with the risen Christ during meals with him.

There are several references in the gospels and Acts to meals as the setting of his appearances (Lk 24:13ff; Jn 21:1-14; Mk 16:14; Acts 1:4,[17] 10:41). We may also add one from the apocryphal *Gospel of the Hebrews*, which speaks of Jesus using a meal to announce his resurrection to James.[18]

One of the most familiar accounts of an appearance at a meal is the story of the journey of two disciples to Emmaus in Luke 24. On Easter Sunday the risen Jesus suddenly joined the two disciples on the road, while they were probably returning to their homes after the Passover, but they did not know that it was Jesus, for "their eyes were kept from recognizing him" (24:16). They were in despair over "the things" that had happened in Jerusalem during the feast (24:18). When Jesus told them that it was necessary "that the Christ should suffer these things and enter into his glory" (24:19) they still did not recognize him, nor were they helped by his interpretation of the scriptures. Only at the breaking of bread were their eyes opened, and as soon as they saw that this was Jesus "he vanished out of their sight" (24:31). At the moment he manifested himself he departed from them. Then they recalled how their hearts had burned while he opened the scriptures to them. At the meal they recognized and experienced the risen Christ as living and present. Upon their return to Jerusalem, they reported to the eleven "how he was known to them in the breaking of the bread" (24:35).

This story is narrated in such a way as to convey the experience of the disciples as well as instruct Christians about the true meaning of the crucifixion and resurrection. The fact that it is found only in the Gospel of St Luke is not sufficient reason to suppose it to be only the creation of one particular evangelist. There is other material in this gospel that we do not find elsewhere (2:19, 51; 7:11-17; 8:1-3; 10:1f; 23:27-31, etc.). It has been argued that here in Luke 24 we have a memory of what happened that was preserved in "private tradition," which

---

[17]Reading συναλιζόμενος as "while eating with them" or "When he had been at table with them" (JB) instead of "while staying with them" (RSV) or "While he was in their company" (NEB).

[18]See above, 89.

Luke drew upon and incorporated into the public apostolic tradition.[19]

The Emmaus episode reflects the liturgical atmosphere of the primitive Church. The structure of the narrative is liturgical: Christ took bread, blessed, broke and gave it to the disciples. At the early eucharistic gatherings the faithful would ask what Jesus did on particular occasions and what he said. Eyewitnesses would recount what they had seen and heard. The words and deeds of Christ were often remembered and transmitted in the setting of liturgical meetings. After readings from the scriptures, the disciples would interpret them in the light of the life, death and resurrection of Christ. All this would be crowned with the breaking of bread, with communion in the crucified and glorified Christ. The liturgical atmosphere of the Emmaus story is particularly conveyed with the phrase "the breaking of the bread" (24:35), which elsewhere St Luke uses to designate the early eucharist (see Acts 2:42, 46; 20:7, 11; 27:35). Yet it is doubtful that St Luke looked upon this meal at Emmaus as an actual eucharist. It belongs to the period between the resurrection and Pentecost, and the eucharist could be realized only after the descent of the Spirit. The Emmaus story, however, was told and developed in the liturgical context of the primitive Church, and we may regard it as a summary of the gospel of the resurrection, for it presents the empty tomb and the resurrected Lord and points to the eucharist as the ever-present evidence of the resurrection.[20]

The meal described by St John at which Jesus revealed himself to seven of his disciples by the Sea of Tiberias (Jn 21:1-14) also has liturgical characteristics. The risen Christ himself offered the meal. He "took the bread and gave it to them, and so with the fish" (21:13). According to the gospel account the disciples provided neither the bread nor the fish, although they had just caught "a hundred and fifty-three of them"

[19]On Lk 24, see P. Benoit, *The Passion and Resurrection of Jesus Christ* (New York: Herder and Herder, 1969) 276f; and Jacques Dupont, "The Meal at Emmaus," in J. Delorme et al., *The Eucharist in the New Testament: A Symposium* (Baltimore: Helicon Press, 1964) 114.

[20]The eucharistic significance of this episode is also present in the icon of the meal at Emmaus. See plate 5.

(21:11). In some mysterious way, they found the bread and fish already prepared on a charcoal fire before they even left the boat. The food that Christ distributes here to his disciples points again to the eucharist, and this meal was presented in early Christian art as a symbol of the eucharist. The same is the case with the feeding of the multitude with five barley loaves and two fish (Jn 6:9; Mk 6:38). Christ is "the bread of life" (Jn 6:35), and the fish became a sign both of Christ and of the eucharist.

Both accounts of appearances at meals, at Emmaus and by the Sea of Tiberias, imply more than recognition of Jesus. The risen Christ has offered himself for the life of his disciples. Neither Luke nor John use eucharistic language in these accounts to necessarily tell us that these meals were the eucharist, but they did connect them with it. As Christ appeared and was present at the meals, so he is present in the eucharist of the Church. At Emmaus Christ vanished suddenly, but now he is remembered, present and recognized in the eucharist. The presence of Christ in the midst of the community, the blessing, the giving of the Spirit and forgiveness that St John describes in 20:19-23 also points to a liturgical setting, and the second appearance to the disciples he records is characteristically introduced with the words: "eight days later, his disciples were again in the house" (20:26). The disciples gathered together on the eighth day, which at the time of the writing of the gospels was undoubtedly a special day of Christian liturgical celebration.

Meals are found as the setting of important meetings between God and man already in the Old Testament. In the account of Genesis 18:1-15, where "the Lord appeared" to Abraham by the oaks of Mamre, the patriarch sets a lavish table for the three heavenly messengers who reveal to him that his wife Sarah will bear a son, whose birth is a sign of the first covenant. It is significant for our purposes here that, although this encounter is most often seen as pointing to the Holy Trinity, the iconography of the Church also sees it as pointing to the eucharist: the outline of the three angels forms the shape of a chalice.[21] At this meal of the old covenant Abraham feeds his heavenly guests. In Isaiah 25:6ff, however, which describes the messianic banquet in the age to come, when the Lord "will swallow up death for ever" (25:8), it is God himself who offers the feast.

We have many accounts of Jesus sitting at meals with his followers, and with sinners too, in the New Testament. We can divide all these meals into three groups: those of Christ's public ministry, those of the post-resurrection period, and those of the Church. The meals that took place in the forty days between the resurrection and the ascension serve as a bridge between the meals of Christ's public life and those of the Church; they refer to meals of the past while anticipating the eucharistic meals of the future.

The meals of the public ministry of Jesus express more than the idea of peace and brotherhood. At them forgiveness is given and salvation is offered. For this reason they constitute one of the most revealing aspects of his ministry.[22] The gospel of life is manifested in the most ordinary situations of human life, such as having a meal. Jesus ate with those who were still in their sins, not waiting for their repentance before associating with them. The Pharisee, in contrast, would accept the repentant sinner, and the pious would prefer the company of the righteous, but Jesus received sinners and ate with them (Lk 15:2). These meals were ordinary meals, but their significance transcended this. They were also signs that the kingdom of God had already been introduced with the coming of the Messiah. There was also a note of foreboding, the shadow of the cross, hanging over these meals, because those who considered themselves to be righteous were shocked that Jesus displayed so much freedom in associating with sinners.

Jesus also presented the coming of the kingdom in terms of

---

[21]See plate 1.

[22]"Why does he eat with tax collectors and sinners?" (Mk 2:16) This sharing of meals with those who have been ostracized "was not a simple breach of etiquette on the part of the individual, it was a clear defiance of both the regulations concerning purity and the ordinances which prescribed the penance required of such violators of the law for restoration into the religious and social community." Gustaf Aulen, *Jesus in Contemporary Historical Research* (Philadelphia: Fortress Press, 1976) 60.

meals and feasting. He proclaimed that those who are hungry now are blessed, for they "shall be satisfied" (Lk 6:21). Before instituting the eucharist, the evangelist Luke records the following words of Jesus: "I have earnestly desired to eat this passover with you before I suffer; for I tell you I shall not eat it until it is fulfilled in the kingdom of God" (22:15-16), and "I shall not drink of the fruit of the vine until the kingdom of God comes" (22:18). Two other evangelists, St Matthew (26:29) and St Mark (14:25), put this last saying after the institution of the eucharist. The order of St Luke appears to be the original, and his arrangement is highly significant. If taken in connection with the account of the eucharist which follows, the future meal Jesus speaks of will have its source in the Last Supper.[23] The last meal stands out as a type for future messianic banquets.

After the crucifixion, in remembrance of the Last Supper, the disciples gathered "to eat the meal at which the risen Christ appeared to them."[24] Those chosen from the beginning are now introduced to the mystery of the resurrection at meals. They are given new knowledge which could only have been hoped for in the pre-resurrection period; their eyes are finally opened. These meals indicate that the disciples are forgiven for abandoning Jesus at the time of his suffering on the cross and that they are readmitted to a new kind of fellowship. The post-resurrection, pre-Pentecost meals are perceptible signs of forgiveness and reincorporation, but above all, together with the empty tomb they form the foundation for faith in the resurrection (Acts 10:39-41).[25] The presence of the risen Christ at these meals was a source of gladness, but these meals also allude to the eucharist, to a new form of his presence. The ancient eucharistic prayer "Our Lord, come!" (μαράνα θά, 1 Cor 16:22) links the remembrance of the Last Supper and the appearances of Christ at meals with the joy of his coming

[23]F. X. Durrwell, *The Resurrection: A Biblical Study* (New York: Sheed and Ward, 1960) 323.

[24]Oscar Cullmann, *Early Christian Worship*, Studies in Biblical Theology, 1st series, 10 (London: SCM Press, 1953) 18.

[25]See Victor Warnach, "Symbol and Reality in the Eucharist," in Pierre Benoit et al., eds., *The Breaking of Bread*, Concilium, 40 (New York: Paulist Press, 1969) 82-105.

and making himself present in the eucharist. The same Lord who appeared to them is now present again in his body, which is the Church.

The accounts of the appearances of the risen Christ at meals are concrete and free of apocalyptic images. There are no signs to watch that would indicate the hour of his coming; he does not appear with the clouds of heaven. The simplicity and clarity of the narratives is well suited to the intensity and purity of the experience of the disciples. They are convinced that Jesus triumphed over death.

Jesus appeared at the meals, but whether he ate with the disciples or not is not always explicitly stated. St John does not say that he did, while St Luke makes it clear that he ate a piece of broiled fish in the presence of the disciples (Lk 24:42-43). According to some accounts he actually ate and according to others he did not and had no need to. Both types of narratives may be found sometimes in the same gospel. There are also passages in the book of Acts that indicate that the risen Christ ate with his disciples (1:4, 10:41). The fathers of the Church stress that the risen Christ did not eat because he needed food, but to convince his disciples that he was really risen from the dead. For the same purpose he showed them the "print of the nails" in his hands, that they may know that it was "the Crucified One Himself, and that another rose not in His stead."[26] The fathers called what took place here a matter of "condescension" (see also Ph 2:6f). By eating he demonstrated that he was not a ghost but had been bodily resurrected. He appeared to convince his disciples that it was he, the same Jesus who called, trained and died for them, who now ate with them.

Different Manners of Appearances

The risen Christ appeared to his disciples not in only one location but wherever they happened to be, in Jerusalem or in Galilee, in a room with the door shut or in an open space by

[26]John Chrysostom, *Homilies on St. John* 87, in **NPNF** 14:328.

the Sea of Galilee. His presence is not limited to any definite
place, and the form of his appearances differs. Each manifestation of Christ is unique as an event as well as in its form.

When Jesus appeared to Mary Magdalene, she presumably
tried to take hold of his feet, and Jesus instructed her: "Do not
hold me" (Jn 20:17). The story of his appearance to Mary
has its psychological as well as theological characteristics. The
account of John 20:1-18 conveys the anxiety, sorrow and joy
of Mary in such a straightforward way as to strongly suggest
that behind it is a firsthand, eyewitness account.[27] Having recognized Jesus, she throws herself at his feet. The context of John
20 determines the theological import of the words "Do not
hold me" or "Stop touching me" (μή μου ἅπτου), "for I
have not yet ascended to the Father." Jesus then asks her to go
tell his "brethren" of his ascension (Jn 20:17), and, according
to this gospel, on the evening of that same day he appears to
the disciples and confers on them the Holy Spirit (20:22). We
shall be discussing the ascension and the giving of the Spirit, as
well as the timing of the New Testament record, in a later
chapter.[28]

A week later, Christ appeared again to the disciples, now
including Thomas, who had been absent from the first appearance and doubted that the disciples had seen the Lord. Although Christ had forbidden Mary Magdalene to touch him,
he now says to Thomas: "Put your finger here, and see my
hands; and put out your hand, and place it in my side; do not
be faithless, but believing" (Jn 20:27). There are different
meanings behind the invitation to Thomas to touch Christ and
the order to Mary not to do so. Thomas, one of the twelve, had
to be convinced that Jesus really rose from the dead. Also,
Christ spoke to Thomas after he had ascended to the Father.
It is in this perspective that St John records the encounter with
both Mary and with Thomas. The text does not tell us whether

---

[27]Christ's saying to Mary Magdalene in Jn 20:17 "has a dramatic value
in the story quite independent of its theological import," and this story as a
whole "has something indefinably first-hand about it. It stands in any case
alone. There is nothing quite like it in the Gospels. Is there anything quite
like it in all ancient literature?" Dodd, "The Appearances of the Risen Christ,"
18f.

[28]See below, chapter 8, " 'Now is the Son of Man Glorified.' "

Thomas did touch him, but it does say that the doubter became a believer and confessed his faith in the resurrection: "My Lord and my God!" (20:28)

It is quite possible that the author of the longer ending of the Gospel of Mark, who uses the expression "in another form" (ἐν ἑτέρᾳ μορφῇ, 16:12), had in mind the different manners of the appearances and disappearances of the risen Christ.[29] His presence cannot be formalized; he appears and disappears in different ways, according to his own initiative, exercising the transcendent freedom of a new level of existence. This fact may have added to the differences between the various reports given by the evangelists of the post-resurrection appearances. Our language is inadequate to convey or describe events that transcend space and time, things that are "beyond our seeing, things beyond our hearing, things beyond our imagining, all prepared by God for those who love him" (1 Cor 2:9). Whatever the place and manner of appearance Jesus chose, the disciples he appeared to recognized him, and all without exception believed in him. Nobody remained in doubt, and all became witnesses to the resurrection.

Christ once came to the disciples in a closed room, with the doors shut (Jn 20:19, 26). He comes to Paul under completely different circumstances. The revelation of the risen Christ to St Paul is narrated no less than three times in the book of Acts. This appearance brings about his call and conversion, which led to the spread of the Christian movement throughout the known world. The earliest written references we have to an appearance of the risen Christ are those we find in Paul's letters to this appearance. For these reasons, this particular appearance will be the subject of the next chapter.

---

[29]Taylor, on Mk 16:12. The Gospel of St Mark may have ended with 16:8, for some important manuscripts do not include the so-called "longer ending" (16:9-20). This longer ending nevertheless is regarded by the Church as canonical, inspired, and possessing apostolic authority.

6

"He Appeared to Me":
The Road to Damascus

"Last of all, as to one untimely born [τῷ ἐκτρώματι] he appeared also to me," writes St Paul to the Corinthians (1 Cor 15:8). In several of his epistles Paul speaks about his experience on the road to Damascus or refers to it. In this case we have his own testimony, the only firsthand written account of an appearance of Jesus after his resurrection. The word Paul uses for himself—ἔκτρωμα—also conveys the meaning of "an object of horror and disgust," or a monster.[1] It implies that at the moment of the appearance Paul was not worthy of it, for he had persecuted the Church of God (1 Cor 15:9). Yet he puts his own experience on the same level with the experiences of Peter and the others in the post-resurrection period of appearances. He was what he became by the grace of God, not because he deserved to be chosen, and "his grace toward me," St Paul asserts, "was not in vain" (1 Cor 15:10).

The Conversion of Paul and its Meaning

Conversion has been defined as "the reorientation of the soul of an individual, his deliberate turning from indifference or from an earlier form of piety to another, or turning which

[1]Richard Kugelman, "The First Letter to the Corinthians," in Raymond E. Brown et al., eds., *Jerome Biblical Commentary* [JBC] (Englewood Cliffs, N.J.: Prentice-Hall, 1968) 51:83.

implies a consciousness that a great change is involved, that the old was wrong and the new is right."[2] This description of conversion covers many examples of turnings in early Christianity and in later times, but it does not describe the conversion of St Paul. To bring this point out more clearly, let us first examine two models of conversion in history that are very well known and documented—the cases of Augustine and Luther—and then contrast them with the conversion of Paul.

Augustine's conversion has been characterized as a "moral conversion," for Augustine craved the "reorientation" from the life he was living to another, which he finally found by accepting Christianity.[3] He actually went through many "conversions," through a process that took many years to complete. Augustine was converted to Christianity at a time when society was already feeling the strong influence of the Christian Church, during the process of the Christianization of pagan society. His mother, Monica, was a member of the Church, and his father, though still outside the Church, did not object to his son's baptism. Throughout his childhood and adolescence Christianity was at the back of his mind, causing an inner ferment as he moved toward and away from it.[4]

Another celebrated conversion was that of Martin Luther, which has been called a "spiritual conversion."[5] In his struggle to overcome despair and to attain a new relationship with a living and gracious God, he experienced extreme dissatisfaction with himself as well as with the life of the Church around him.

[2]Arthur D. Nock, *Conversion: The Old and New in Religion from Alexander the Great to Augustine of Hippo* (Oxford: University Press, 1952) 7. Nock, however, insists that the conversion of Paul stands by itself (254).

[3]Philippe H. Menoud, "Revelation and Tradition: The Influence of Paul's Conversion on his Theology," *Interpretation* 7:2 (1953) 131.

[4]Nock, *Conversion*, 262. Augustine's conversion "took years to complete." See Sallie McFague, "Conversion: Life on the Edge of the Raft," *Interpretation* 32:3 (1978) 261ff. Augustine's baptism was postponed to a later time in his life not because of the objections of his pagan father but because of his Christian mother, who wanted her son to enjoy himself before his baptism. She thus reflected a very superstitious practice of postponing baptism, which entered the Church along with the countless number of pagans who flocked to it after it became the official religious body of the empire. See Joachim Jeremias, *Infant Baptism in the First Four Centuries* (London: SCM Press, 1960) 95.

[5]Menoud, 131.

Luther's period of dissatisfaction and doubt prepared him for the moment of decision. His was a conversion within the Church, which he now saw clearly in a new light, as a "newborn" Christian.

Compared with these conversions, or with any that we find in the book of Acts or in the subsequent history of the Church, Paul's conversion stands by itself. He writes to the Galatians that before his conversion he had "advanced in Judaism beyond many of my own age among my people, so extremely zealous was I for the traditions of my fathers" (1:14), and he does not suggest here that he regretted having done so, or that he was dissatisfied with his efforts to live according to the demands of the law. Again, while summarizing his previous life for the Philippians, he tells them that while he was living according to the way of life of Judaism he had considered it a gain; only after the call of Christ "whatever gain I had, I counted as loss for the sake of Christ" (3:7). These two passages serve as a warning not to reduce the experience that Paul had on the road to Damascus to discontent with his traditional faith. In his own understanding, his conversion came about not because he wished to remove the heavy burden of life under the law and to find a new freedom. He was not converted because he thought that "the old was wrong" and "the new was right." There is no evidence that Paul experienced anguish, despair or tension while he was a Pharisee, nor was he yearning to find something to believe in.

Krister Stendahl, in his pertinent essay "The Apostle Paul and the Introspective Conscience of the West," has particularly stressed the "drastic difference" between St Paul and Luther and warned against interpreting Paul's experience on the basis of Luther's. Paul is often misunderstood by those who see in him the discontent with his spiritual state that preceded the conversion of Luther. Paul sinned in the past by persecuting the Christian Church, and therefore, he tells the Corinthians, he is "unfit to be called an apostle" (1 Cor 15:9). Yet he immediately adds that he made up for this terrible sin: "But by the grace of God I am what I am, and his grace toward me was not in vain" (15:10). Paul did not suffer from a "plagued conscience." He believed that the Lord had approved him, and

"this robust man is not shaken but strengthened by his awareness of a final judgment which has not come yet," as he com-
municates in his epistles, particularly 2 Corinthians 5:10ff.[6]

St Paul did not consider belonging to the people of Israel
a loss. His new membership in the body of Christ he ascribed
to God, who revealed his Son to him "in order that I might
preach him among the Gentiles" (Ga 1:16). He speaks of
the "revelation" of the risen Christ, emphasizing the external
character of the appearance (Ga 1:12).[7] The glory that Paul
saw on the road to Damascus was the glory of the age to
come, which Paul experienced already in this age. And because of this experience the apostle counted "everything as
loss because of the surpassing worth of knowing Christ Jesus
my Lord. For his sake I have suffered the loss of all things,
and count them as refuse, in order that I may gain Christ and
be found in him, not having a righteousness of my own, based
on law, but that which is through faith in Christ, the righteousness from God that depends on faith" (Ph 3:8-9).

Some interpreters have pointed to Romans 7:7-25, which
they regard as autobiographical, as an indication of inner
tensions experienced by Paul prior to his conversion. "I was
once alive apart from the law, but when the commandment
came, sin revived and I died; the very commandment which
promised life proved to be death to me" (7:9-10). This has
been interpreted as an allusion to Paul's life prior to receiving
the commandment to live the life of a Jew.[8] Also taken to be
autobiographical, referring either to Paul's life as a Pharisee

[6]Krister Stendahl, *Paul among Jews and Gentiles* (Philadelphia: Fortress
Press, 1976) 12, 89ff. In this same essay, which is included in the book just
cited (78-96), Stendahl notes in passing: "Judging at least from a superficial
survey of the preaching of the Churches of the East from olden times to the
present, it is striking how their homiletical tradition is either one of doxology
or meditative mysticism or exhortation—but it does not deal with the plagued
conscience in the way in which one came to do so in the Western Churches"
(85).

[7]In the letters of St Paul the word "revelation" means "an objective world-
changing event through which God in his sovereign action has inaugurated a
new aeon," writes Gunther Bornkamm in *Paul* (New York: Harper & Row,
1971) 21.

[8]See, among many others, Wayne A. Meeks, ed., *The Writings of St. Paul:
Norton Critical Edition* (New York: W. W. Norton, 1972) 79.

or possibly to his experience as a Christian, is the passage "For I do not do the good I want, but the evil I do not want is what I do. Now if I do what I do not want, it is no longer I that do it, but sin which dwells within me" (7:19-20).[9] These passages do not seem to accord with those from Galatians and Philippians that we have already cited, describing Paul's serenity and certainty when he was living as a Pharisee. Nevertheless, most recent interpreters discard the theories that these passages are autobiographical and reject efforts to make a "young Luther" out of Paul on the basis of them.[10]

What we have in Romans 7:9-10 is not a summary of St Paul's experience under the law, but rather an interpretation of Genesis 2:4-3:24, the story of Adam's relation to God and his fall. The commandment "which promised life" (Rm 7:10) and which the apostle had in mind when he wrote this chapter was the one given to Adam: "And the Lord God commanded the man, saying, 'You may freely eat of every tree of the garden; but of the tree of the knowledge of good and evil you shall not eat, for in the day that you eat of it you shall die'" (Gn 2:16-17). The serpent, approaching the woman with the question "Did God say, 'You shall not eat of any tree in the garden?'" (3:1), engaged Eve in a conversation about God's demand, which the serpent misrepresented, and in this way brought about the fall of Adam and Eve and their expulsion from paradise. In Romans 7:19-20 as well, the "I" is not autobiographical but a corporate "I," standing for all mankind. By using the term "I," Paul gives in summary form what happened to humanity without Christ. What we have in Romans 7 then is a perspective on the history of salvation, not an autobiographical commentary.

---

[9]Stendahl finds it "striking that 'I', the *ego,* is not simply identified with Sin and Flesh." Paul's "argument is one of acquittal of the ego, not one of utter contrition" (92-3).

[10]Joseph A. Fitzmyer, "The Letter to the Romans," in JBC 53:74. Paul's use of "I" is a "stylistic figure." He could have written "man" or "someone" instead of "I." In the words of another Pauline scholar, the exegesis which sees in Rm 7 a description of Paul's inner struggle "is now relegated to the museum of exegetical misinterpretation." Beda Rigaux, *Letters of St. Paul: Modern Studies* (Chicago: Franciscan Herald Press, 1968) 50.

The Appearance and Visions

For St Paul the experience near Damascus was unique,
incomparable to any of his other experiences. He makes a
clear distinction between the appearance of Christ to him and
all other spiritual experiences he had later in the course of his
missionary labors. About these other experiences he is reticent,
but not about the appearance near Damascus. He never uses
the word "vision" in reference to his conversion, but he does
use it in describing other spiritual experiences. He tells us,
for example:

> I must boast; there is nothing to be gained by it, but
> I will go on to visions [ὀπτασίας] and revelations
> [ἀποκαλύψεις] of the Lord. I know a man in Christ
> who fourteen years ago was caught up to the third
> heaven . . . And I know that this man was caught up
> into Paradise . . . and he heard things that cannot be
> told, which man may not utter. (2 Cor 12:1-4)

St Luke also records visions that Paul had: "And a vision
[ὅραμα] appeared to Paul in the night: a man of Macedonia
was standing beseeching him and saying, 'Come over to
Macedonia and help us' " (Acts 16:9); and on another occa-
sion: "And the Lord said to Paul one night in a vision
[δι' ὁράματος], 'Do not be afraid, but speak and do not
be silent' " (Acts 18:9). These "visions" do not belong in
the same category as the appearances of Christ either to his
disciples or to Paul. With the words "Last of all . . . he
appeared also to me" (1 Cor 15:8), Paul separates this experience from any later visions or revelations, and seems to indicate that the privileged period of post-resurrection appearances
of the risen Christ is ended with his Damascus experience.

Sight is a central element in Paul's experience on the road
to Damascus. He emphasizes that he has "seen Jesus our Lord"
(1 Cor 9:1). Skeptical historians and theologians have attempted to interpret the verb "see" (ὁράω) here as meaning
that the apostle experienced the presence of Christ without

actually seeing him. In other words, they suggest that the term St Paul uses does not have a visual quality, and the "vision" of Damascus is nothing more than a release of the subconscious and the projection into the conscious mind of repressed ideas or facts.[11] But this is not at all implied, and it is not the proper sense of the verb "to see" that Paul uses in 1 Corinthians 9:1. Paul's claim is that he has seen the risen Christ with his own eyes.

In 2 Corinthians the apostle describes his conversion in terms of a heavenly light, which is the glory of God "who has shone in our hearts to give the light of the knowledge of the glory of God in the face of Christ" (4:6). For St Paul, this light was the visible manifestation of God. For three days after his conversion Paul could not see (Acts 9:9). The cause of blindness was not simply the light, but the "brightness" or glory (ἡ δόξα, Acts 22:11) of the light, and this glory was for Paul the most distinctive aspect of his experience.[12]

The conversion of St Paul was of such importance for the primitive Church that St Luke records it three times in his highly selective book of Acts. In all three accounts the dialogue between the risen Christ and the persecutor of the Church is essentially the same.

> Now as he journeyed he approached Damascus, and suddenly a light from heaven flashed about him. And he fell to the ground and heard a voice saying to him, "Saul, Saul, why do you persecute me?" And he said, "Who are you, Lord?" And he said, "I am Jesus, whom you are persecuting; but rise and enter the city, and you will be told what you are to do." (Acts 9:3-6; cf 22:6ff and 26:13ff)

[11]M. Goguel, for instance, expressed it in the following way: "The conversion was preconditioned by a deep anterior ferment in his subliminal ego wherein the Christian claims concerning the resurrection of the Master and the new moral ideal proclaimed by Jesus had made slow headway, while, at the same time, in his conscious mind, they were repressed by the axiom of the curse uttered against the cross and by attachment to the traditional religious form." *La Foi à la Résurrection dans le Christianisme primitif* (Paris, 1933) 429; quoted in Rigaux, 47.

[12]David M. Stanley, *The Apostolic Church in the New Testament* (Westminster, Md.: Newman Press, 1965) 303.

Unlike the appearances we discussed previously, Christ here makes himself known to one who was persecuting those who belonged to "this Way" (22:4) and identifies himself with the persecuted Christian community. The revelation given to Paul, according to these reports, was presented as something visible as well as audible. In none of the three accounts that we find in Acts is there any support whatsoever for the view of this revelation as a subjective vision confined to Paul's inner experience. All our written records exclude this theory. What is unmistakably stressed in these three accounts is the same thing that Paul himself bore witness to in his letters: that the vision was not subjective but an appearance, and if we choose to use the term "vision" then we must qualify it as an exterior vision.

Those who accompanied Paul to Damascus were also affected by this experience, which again indicates that it could not have been just a subjective experience. Our records, it is true, are not unanimous as to what happened to them and what their reaction was at the moment of Christ's appearance to Paul. In Acts 9:7 St Luke reports: "The men who were traveling with him stood speechless, hearing the voice but seeing no one." In Acts 22:9, however, as Paul was defending himself before the people, addressing them in Hebrew (Aramaic), he stated: "Now those who were with me saw the light but did not hear the voice of the one who was speaking to me." Again, when Paul was defending himself before Herod Agrippa II, the great-grandson of Herod the Great, he reported that "At midday, O king, I saw on the way a light from heaven, brighter than the sun, shining round me and those who journeyed with me" (Acts 26:13). Did they see the light or not? Did they hear the voice or not?

As we see, there are discrepancies in these three accounts. However, these disagreements themselves underline the one central and most important fact—that the revelation was given to Paul and not to his companions. All three records are unanimous in this. Paul was given the vision, and he responded and understood its meaning and consequences. Those who were with him were able to testify to the objective, exterior character of the appearance, but they were confused and did not understand what was really happening, for the revelation was not given to them, Christ did not appear to them. They saw the light and heard the voice without perceiving the meaning or importance of what was occurring.

"He Appeared" (ὤφθη)

In the context of what St Paul says in Galatians 1, the expression "revelation of Jesus Christ" (1:12) implies not simply a "revelation given *by* Jesus Christ," but a "revelation which *is* Jesus Christ himself." It is better in this case to speak of *who* was revealed to Paul than *what* was revealed. Christ, who overcame death, revealed himself to the persecutor of his Church. Paul has "seen" the glorified Christ (1 Cor 9:1), for he "appeared" (ὤφθη) or "made himself known" to him (1 Cor 15:8). This crucial expression ὤφθη, which appears in the credal statement of 1 Corinthians 15 as well as in other passages of the New Testament (Lk 24:34; Acts 9:17, 13:31, 26:16), points to the external, objective character of the Easter event as well as to the presence of the risen Christ before Paul outside Damascus.

The word ὤφθη, which in 1 Corinthians 15:5-8 is usually translated as "he appeared" (RSV, JB, NEB) or "he was seen" (KJV), is a passive form of the verb ὁράω (I see). This passive form is used "mostly of beings that make their appearance in a supernatural manner always with dative of the persons to whom they appear."[13] Such usage we find in Luke 24:34—he "has appeared to Simon" (ὤφθη Σίμωνι)— as well as in 1 Corinthians 15:5-8. In another context, ὤφθη refers to the triumphant Christ who appears to the angelic powers, who was "seen by angels" (1 Tm 3:16), and in Hebrews 9:28 the term is used in connection with Christ at his second coming, his parousia: "when he appears a second time, it will not be to deal with sin but to reward with salvation those who are waiting for him."[14]

[13]William F. Arndt and F. Wilbur Gingrich, *A Greek-English Lexicon of the New Testament and Other Early Christian Literature* (Chicago: University Press, 1957) 581-2.

[14]This verb is also used in the Septuagint version of the Old Testament, in

On this basis, Xavier Léon-Dufour has argued that the term "appearance" should not be replaced by the words "vision" or "experience," for these words "describe the phenomenon on the basis of the subject who sees or experiences, whereas the biblical writers are seeking to emphasize the intervention of Christ himself." The verb ὤφθη in 1 Corinthians 15:5-8 should therefore be translated as "he showed himself." In the accounts of the appearances the emphasis is upon Christ and not upon any mystical exaltation of the disciples. Their experience of Christ is not the product of an "over-active faith or a fertile imagination," but of divine action.[15] The risen Christ takes the initiative. He appears to whom he will, exercising his sovereign freedom. The word ὤφθη expresses both faith in the resurrection of Christ as well as rejection by the Church of every attempt that has been made throughout the centuries to reduce the appearances of Christ to subjective human experiences. They are rather events in history that transcend human perceptions.[16]

In a sermon delivered in the synagogue in Antioch in Pisidia, Paul again used the term "he appeared" with reference to Christ's post-resurrection appearances. "God raised him from the dead, and for many days he appeared to those who had accompanied him from Galilee to Jerusalem" (Acts 13:30-31). As God is the subject of the verb "to raise," so God is the one who made Christ manifest (Acts 10:40). Thus, neither the resurrection nor the Christophanies are assigned to man's perceptions, but to God's initiative. By

reference to persons "who freely allow themselves to be seen" (Ex 23:15, 34:20). It specifically is used in divine epiphanies: "God emerges from his radical invisibility and allows himself, his 'glory' or his 'angel' to be seen" (Gn 12:7; Ex 3:2f). G. O'Collins, *The Easter Jesus* (London: Darton, Longman and Todd, 1973) 8.

[15]Xavier Léon-Dufour, *Resurrection and the Message of Easter* (New York: Holt, Rinehart and Winston, 1975) 42f.

[16]See J. D. G. Dunn, *Jesus and the Spirit* (Philadelphia: Westminster Press, 1975) 105, where he quotes K. H. Rengstorf about the profound implications of "he appeared" in the resurrection references. This term expresses "the earliest available protest of a Christianity still on the soil of the early Palestinian community against the attempt to strip the Easter event of its objective character and to transform it from an affair of God into an affair of the disciples."

the vocabulary they use as well as in their lives and in their missionary activity, the evangelists and St Paul express their conviction that the appearances of the risen Christ belong to transcendent, objective, external reality.

There is one passage in St Paul's Epistle to the Galatians that might be taken as an indication that what he saw at the time of his conversion had something to do with his inner life. The external, visual character of the appearance seems to be toned down here. God "was pleased to reveal his Son to me [ἐν ἐμοί], in order that I might preach him among the Gentiles" (Ga 1:16). The more usual meaning of the words ἐν ἐμοί would be *"in* me," not *"to* me," and some exegetes argue that this phrase here should be rendered "in me." But even this expression would not contradict the external, visible character of the appearance, so strongly indicated in other passages of St Paul. This passage in Galatians adds another dimension, of a visible manifestation that is internalized, which is present but not spelled out in other passages dealing with Paul's conversion. It would have been no conversion at all if the apostle had not appropriated what was given to him on the road to Damascus and made it his own.[17] It would not have been complete without the inner illumination—the response—which followed the external manifestation—the revelation. Paul also experienced Christ as an inner power, which directed and transformed his life. This Christ who loved him and gave himself for him, as Paul himself expresses it, appeared to him on the road to Damascus, and after that he was able to experience Christ as living in him (Ga 2:20).

Conversion: Jesus as the Promised Messiah

The conversion of Paul was not a conversion from a life without God to a life with God. Paul had believed in the God

---

[17]This expression "in me" in Ga 1:16 "reflects the fundamental interior revolution" which the appearance of Christ produced in Paul, writes Alfred Wikenhauser. This scholar continues that Christ "revealed himself as a personal power with a profound influence on Paul's life," and "this revelation

of Israel, and he did not reject Him after becoming a follower of Christ. Yet this Damascus experience revealed the God of his people to be the "Father of our Lord Jesus Christ" (2 Cor 1:3; Rm 15:6; Col 1:3; Eph 1:3). For Paul, "Father" has become God's proper name, newly revealed in his Son.[18]

The appearance on the road to Damascus led Paul to recognize that the crucified Jesus was the Messiah of his people. Before his conversion Paul was convinced that this Jesus could not have been the Messiah, because he had been rejected by the authorities of the people of God and seemingly by God himself. For Paul, being a Pharisee, Christ's crucifixion was a "stumbling block," an "offense" (σκάνδαλον, 1 Cor 1:23), for "Cursed be every one who hangs on a tree" (Ga 3:13, quoting Dt 21:23). Now this crucified and risen Christ had "redeemed us from the curse of the law, having become a curse for us" (Ga 3:13). With his conversion he accepts Jesus as the Messiah, and for his sake he becomes "all things to all men" (1 Cor 9:22). Whatever he did, wherever he taught or preached, it was now as a "servant [δοῦλος] of Christ" (Ga 1:10, etc.). He suffers for the sake of the gospel more than any other, for he is put "under necessity" to proclaim it (see 1 Cor 9:16). He was so transformed and led by Christ that he is unwilling and incapable of taking any other course but speaking the truth that was revealed to him. All this was due to the exterior vision he had on the road to Damascus.

The appearance of the risen Lord converted him to a new way of righteousness, one not based on human merits and achievements but on faith in the risen Christ. St Paul does not teach "instant salvation," nor does he see salvation only

was something extraordinary; in the strict sense of the word it was a miracle. But it cannot be simply equated to the fellowship with Christ which, according to Paul, every Christian enjoys." See his *Pauline Mysticism: Christ in the Mystical Teaching of St. Paul* (Edinburgh: Nelson, 1960) 135-6.

[18]"Everywhere in St. Paul and St. John . . . one encounters the word God, one should read, as its sense and as the direction of its address, 'the Father.' This is now God's proper Name. He is 'The Father of our Lord Jesus Christ' in whose manifestation as Son the Name of God was newly revealed." John Courtney Murray, *The Problem of God, Yesterday and Today* (New Haven: Yale University Press, 1964) 27.

as a present reality. He regards salvation as both present and future. He writes that "we are justified" in him, that "we have redemption," that "now is the day of salvation" (Rm 5:1; Eph 1:7; 2 Cor 6:2), and yet there is a promise for the future, for "we wait for the hope of righteousness," we are "sealed for the day of redemption," and therefore let us "put on the breastplate of faith and love, and for a helmet the hope of salvation" (Ga 5:5; Eph 4:30; 1 Th 5:8). Christians, according to St Paul, "are being saved" (σωζομένοις, 1 Cor 1:18), and thus he encourages his readers to "work out your own salvation with fear and trembling" (Ph 2:12).

This leads us to his view of the "last things," or eschatology. As a Pharisee he was committed to the belief that the messianic age belonged exclusively to the future. Now, however, due to the experience outside Damascus, Paul was convinced that the last age, the age to come, had already been inaugurated with the death and resurrection of Jesus of Nazareth. What belongs to the future has become a reality in the past and the source of new life in the present. Christians live in an overlapping of ages. The old has not yet passed away, yet the powers of the age to come are already here. This vision of his mission, rooted in the Damascus experience, determined the whole course of his writing and preaching.

Born in Tarsus, a Hellenistic city, and educated in Jerusalem, Paul knew Greek as well as Hebrew and Aramaic and lived in both traditions, drawing on both for words and images to express what had happened to him outside Damascus. He also drew figures of speech from various aspects of human life and activity to express the height and depth of his experience and message. J. D. G. Dunn has summarized these sources admirably:

> With various metaphors drawn from the law courts (justification), from the slave market (redemption), from warfare (reconciliation), from everyday life (salvation-wholeness, health), from agriculture (sowing, watering, grafting, harvest), from commerce and trade (seal, down payment, building), from religion (cir-

cumcision, baptism, consecration, anointing), and from the major events of life and world history (creation, birth, adoption, marriage, death), he tried to express the new dimension of his own experience and that of his converts.[19]

His experience of conversion gave all these expressions a new color and a new meaning, as he searched for adequate words and images to convey the mystery of Christ.

The Revelation of the Son and Paul's Mission

St Paul emphasizes that he has "seen Jesus our Lord" (1 Cor 9:1) and therefore that he is an apostle of Christ. God "was pleased to reveal his Son to me, in order that I might preach him among the Gentiles" (Ga 1:16). Paul relates his apostolic mission to the very moment of the appearance of Christ, to the moment of his conversion.

On the basis of the apostle's words, then, can we conclude that his conversion and call are indistinguishable, occurring at the same time and place? The texts themselves show that they are inseparable—they cannot be seen as two distinct events in time. They are one in St Paul, and the same holds for the accounts of his conversion in Acts. In one of those accounts, for example, Paul's vocation is revealed along with the appearance of Christ:

> But rise and stand upon your feet; for I have appeared to you for this purpose, to appoint you to serve and bear witness to the things in which you have seen me and to those in which I will appear to you, delivering you from the people and from the Gentiles—to whom I send you to open their eyes. (Acts 26:16-18; cf 9:15 and 22:14-15)

There are some who have argued that Paul's conversion through the external vision given to him and his call to the apostolate did not occur simultaneously. According to them,

[19]Dunn, 308f.

Paul received a revelation regarding his mission to the gentiles not at the very moment of the appearance of Christ outside Damascus but soon afterward. How soon? Nobody can be sure about the precise time and place, but it has been suggested that Paul came to understand his vocation fully only in the course of his missionary activities. As we have pointed out, however, any separation of Paul's vision and conversion from his mission inevitably comes into conflict with the evidence and the witness of St Luke and St Paul himself.

This does not preclude a deepening of his understanding of the revelation and his perception of his mission over the course of time. An example of such a subsequent development might be his allusions to the three great prophets of ancient Israel—Isaiah, Jeremiah and Ezekiel. In Galatians 1:15-16 St Paul alludes unmistakably to the call of Jeremiah (Jr 1:5) and possibly also to Isaiah 49:1, and in Acts 26:16 he refers to the call of Ezekiel (Ez 2:1ff). In these passages he links his call by the risen Christ to the calls of the prophets. Of course his call differs from theirs, in that he received his while he was persecuting the Christian community whereas the prophets were called to exercise their prophetic mission within the covenantal community they were already members of and in which they received their calls. Like them, however, Paul was summoned personally to bear witness to God's holiness, sovereignty, power and glory. By alluding to the prophetic calls, St Paul wanted to underline the place and significance of his own mission in the history of salvation.

The more Paul entered into the mystery of Christ, the more he saw the link between the suffering of Christ and his apostolic ministry, the more he perceived the unity of his conversion and call. With clarity he could see and with profound conviction he could write that both his vocation and his "turning" belong to and are rooted in the moment of the appearance of Christ. The vision and vocation are related as the root is to the tree. Thus, St Paul saw his vocation as being contained in that original vision, yet fully revealed in his contact with the living tradition and in preaching and suffering for the gospel.[20]

---

[20]See an interesting discussion and survey on this point in Rigaux, 60-2.

The vision of Christ that Paul experienced and the tradition of the Church that he received lived together in him and in his work. St Paul's very greatness lies in the fact that revelation and tradition are so intimately united in him. His whole life and teaching refute the supposition that he was the "founder of Christianity," as he has been called. His vision and what he received from the Church were essentially one and the same for him, for the origin of both was Christ.[21] Three years after the conversion he goes to Jerusalem to visit Peter, most probably to get information about Jesus and his public ministry (Ga 1:18). He returns again to Jerusalem fourteen years later (Ga 2:1). Those who were called by Jesus during his ministry in Palestine and to whom the risen Jesus appeared approved Paul's work and treated him as an equal. The pillars of the primitive Church in Jerusalem "added nothing" to the gospel of Paul (Ga 2:6), and instead gave him "the right hand of fellowship" (Ga 2:9).

Throughout his missionary activities St Paul, who became an apostle "not from men nor through man, but through Jesus Christ and God the Father" (Ga 1:1), kept his contacts with Jerusalem. As his writings clearly display, he depended on the sacramental and doctrinal traditions of the primitive Church. St Paul gives us the earliest extant testimony regarding the institution of the eucharist (1 Cor 11:23ff) and the most complete summary of the primitive apostolic preaching (1 Cor 15:3ff). In his epistles he incorporated liturgical hymns from the tradition of the Church (Ph 2:6-11, for example) as well as liturgical formulas (1 Cor 16:22). The gospel that he preached was the same gospel preached by Peter, John and James. The gospel he received and the gospel of the Church's tradition are not two but one, the same gospel of Christ. For Paul, as for the other apostles, the ultimate source and criterion is Christ himself.

[21]Menoud, 141. He states that "Paul was the man who could have created his own movement, as so many Christian leaders did in the course of history from the second century onwards. But Paul did not. He understood that the Gospel is all both revelation and tradition by the very nature of things." See also the clear summary of the consequences of Damascus for St Paul's theology in Joachim Jeremias, "The Key to Pauline Theology," *Expository Times* 76:1 (1964) 27-30.

A man of high rank in the Jewish community, Paul was sent to Damascus as a *shaliah* but became an apostle and δοῦλος of Christ. The Aramaic *shaliah* or Hebrew *shaluah* means a "commissioned emissary" sent out to represent the Palestinian authorities and to act with the power and authority of the sender, and the word belongs to the rabbinic institution. The concept of *shaliah* has been considered by some as a likely source for the concept of the New Testament apostolate, though most contemporary commentators see too many fundamental differences between the two concepts and too little historical evidence to make that connection.[22] St Paul, after having met, seen and heard the risen Christ, now becomes his δοῦλος (servant), and is no longer out to complete only a certain assignment but is sent (ἀποστέλλειν) to proclaim what he has seen and heard: that Christ is risen from the dead, in fulfilment of the prophecies of the Old Testament. Here again we see the unity of Paul's conversion and mission. The appearance to Paul causes him to become Christ's servant and itself determines the nature of his apostolate.

The appearance of the risen Christ to Paul has all the major characteristics of the post-resurrection appearances but at the same time differentiates his conversion from the conversions of the post-Pentecostal period. Paul did not hesitate to put it on the same level with the personal appearances granted to the disciples, who had been trained and taught by Christ during his public ministry. The pillars of the Church in Jerusalem—James, Cephas and John—accepted this appearance for what Paul himself claimed it to be (Ga 2:9). For St Paul the appearance outside Damascus completed and closed the list of post-resurrection Christophanies.

Both St Paul and the evangelist Luke agree fully in distinguishing these appearances from other visions and the gift of the Spirit. They insist that Christ was seen and heard at the time of his appearances, and they strongly indicate the

---

[22]See the article on "The Twelve and the Apostolate," by David M. Stanley and Raymond E. Brown, in JBC 78:174-7. The apostles were missionaries, and this missionary element "fundamentally differentiates the New Testament apostleship from the Jewish *shaliah* institution." K. Rengstorf, "ἀπόστολος," in Gerhard Kittel, ed., *Theological Dictionary of the New Testament,* 10 vols. (Grand Rapids, Mich.: Eerdmans, 1964-1976) 1:431ff.

bodily reality of his resurrection. Neither Paul in his letters nor the evangelists in their gospels try to reduce his presence at these moments to a subjective vision or to a kind of inner dwelling. Both Paul and the evangelists insist that Jesus appeared to them as an external reality, the Son of God raised from the dead.

7

The Bodily Resurrection

"I believe in the resurrection without necessarily believing in the bodily Resurrection," a modern minister is reported to have said.[1] Such a statement is an expression that makes the resurrection of Christ acceptable to the modern mind. It is not consonant with the record of the New Testament, nor with the faith of the Church, however. The whole New Testament witness rests firmly on the conviction that the bodily resurrection did indeed occur. Although it may be hard for us to realize, the bodily resurrection is not just a modern problem but has always presented a challenge to human thinking. Men were often tempted to reduce this New Testament teaching and witness of the primitive Church to forms that would fit their limited human experience.

If the resurrection was not bodily, what else could it be but a manifestation of the "immortality of the soul," which exists outside the body before birth and will continue to exist after death? This ancient philosophical view of the soul was known in the very first centuries of Christianity, was espoused by the gnostics and was fervently attacked by the fathers of the Church as unbiblical. As we shall see, the fathers did not regard the flesh in itself as inherently corruptible, something to be overcome at death, but rather as "resurrectible," capable of salvation as well as destruction.

The entire teaching of St Paul and the fathers of the Church on salvation points to the salvation of body and soul, and would be meaningless if Christ's resurrection had not been a

[1]*Time* (February 16, 1981) 78.

127

bodily resurrection. Before examining their teachings, however, let us briefly summarize some of the gospel witness to
the bodily resurrection.

On the day of Pentecost, Peter stressed that God raised
Jesus up, that it was not possible for Christ to be held by
death (Acts 2:24, 32) and that the Holy One did not see
corruption (2:27, 31). The evangelists in their records also
bore witness to the bodily resurrection. At the time of Christ's
appearance to the women, they "took hold of his feet and
worshiped him" (Mt 28:9). According to another gospel
account, Mary Magdalene wanted to take hold of his feet
but was dissuaded when Christ said to her: "Do not hold me,
for I have not yet ascended to the Father" (Jn 20:17). In
contrast, Thomas was invited to touch him (Jn 20:27). The
mission of Thomas, like that of the other disciples, was to
bear witness to Christ's bodily resurrection. This was what
the historical evidence—the empty tomb and the appearances
—bore witness to.

By attesting to the bodily resurrection, the apostles affirmed the truth of the identity of the incarnate and risen
Christ. It is the body of the historical Jesus which the New
Testament speaks about as resurrected. Christ's resurrection
is not isolated from his previous life—it is its fulfilment. For
the evangelists, the resurrection meant the resurrection of the
body. In this they remained faithful to the traditions they
received, in which the most recognizable and known fact was
the bodily resurrection of Jesus. All the appearances recorded
in the gospels were bodily. It is true that the expression "he
appeared" (ὤφθη) does not by itself indicate a consistent,
identical mode of appearance, but all those to whom Christ
appeared, in whatever mode and under whatever circumstances, testified that the one whom they had seen and heard
before the crucifixion was the same Jesus they saw and heard
after the resurrection.

Body and Flesh in St Paul

St Paul is particularly preoccupied with the nature of the

bodily resurrection in 1 Corinthians 15. He starts the chapter, as we have already seen, with credal statements about the burial, resurrection and appearances of Christ (15:3-8). His death was a death in the flesh, his burial was a burial of the body, and his death and burial together with his later appearances confirm the resurrection of the body. The apostolic proclamation is the proclamation of the bodily resurrection of Christ.[2]

For St Paul, the resurrected Christ is the "first fruits of those who have fallen asleep" (1 Cor 15:20). The apostle Paul sees an intrinsic connection between the resurrection of Christ and the general resurrection that will take place in the future. As the resurrection of Christ was bodily, so the future resurrection will be bodily. But "How are the dead raised? With what kind of body [σώματι] do they come?" (1 Cor 15:35) Paul's answer is that it is "a spiritual body" (σῶμα πνευματικόν, 1 Cor 15:44). The term "body" (σῶμα) is of great significance in 1 Corinthians 15—St Paul's "gospel of resurrection"—and therefore let us attempt to clarify and grasp the meaning of his use of the term.

St Paul uses the term "body" to signify the whole man, not a part of man. Man belongs to Christ in his entirety, just as Christ, in his incarnation, took on human nature in its entirety. In his letter to the Romans, he appeals to the Christians in Rome "to present your bodies [σώματα] as a living sacrifice, holy and acceptable to God, which is your spiritual [λογικήν] worship" (12:1). One modern commentator has pointed out in this passage a "startling combination of what had been heretofore incompatible: on the one hand, Hellenistic spiritualization, and on the other, Hebrew somatic and Christian incarnational views." Paul borrows from Greek religious philosophy the vocabulary of the λογικὴ θυσία (spiritual or reasonable sacrifice) and combines it with the word σῶμα, which so concisely expresses the Semitic concrete view of reality. Bringing together these two ideas, Greek and Semitic, to express the Christian view of existence enables St Paul "to reject the Hellenistic mistrust of matter and

---

[2]See Chrysostom's comments on 1 Cor 15:1-2, in NPNF 12:226ff.

to emphasize two cardinal points of Christian faith: creation and incarnation."[3] The body denotes the totality of man, as in the eucharistic words of Christ: "This is my body [σῶμα]" (Mt 26:26; Mk 14:22; Lk 22:19; 1 Cor 11:24). In his sacrifice on behalf of all mankind, Christ also offers himself in the totality of his person. St Paul is here asking the Roman Christians, in the words of Chrysostom, to present *themselves,* in their entire bodily, physical aspect:

> Let not your eye look upon anything evil, and it has become a sacrifice; let not your tongue speak anything improper, and it has become an offering; let not your hand do any lawless deed, and it has become a whole burnt offering . . .[4]

Centuries after Chrysostom, St Gregory Palamas followed this line of interpretation of Romans 12:1:

> We must then offer to God the passionate part of the soul, living and active, that it may be a living sacrifice . . . How can our living body be offered . . .? [It is offered] when the look in our eyes is gentle . . . when our ears are attentive to the divine teachings, not hearing them only, but, as David says, "remembering the commandments of God to accomplish them" [Ps 103:18] . . . when our tongue, our hands and our feet are at the service of the divine will.[5]

Paul, Chrysostom and Gregory all refer to the total person in physical, bodily form—the same total physical person who was consecrated to God in baptism. The totality of the human being—not only body but body and soul together—is offered in a bodily baptism, and the resurrection of the baptized will also be bodily (see Rm 6:4-5).

---

[3]Robert J. Daly, *The Origin of the Christian Doctrine of Sacrifice* (Philadelphia: Fortress Press, 1978) 64.

[4]From his *Homilies on Romans* 20, NPNF 11:496.

[5]Cited in John Meyendorff, *A Study of Gregory Palamas* (Crestwood, N.Y.: SVS Press, 1964) 144-5.

The body is a solid reality for St Paul, and his own body, moreover, is not his enemy—his goal is mastery over it (1 Cor 9:26-27). In our central passage—1 Corinthians 15:35-44—however, Paul also uses another term: flesh (σάρξ). He begins with the term "body," but in the middle of the discussion exchanges it for the term "flesh." "With what kind of body do they come?" (15:35) is the question of those who rejected the future bodily resurrection, and Paul answers it with the analogy of sowing and harvesting: after the seed is sown "God gives it a body [σῶμα] as he has chosen, and to each kind of seed its own body" (15:38). But in the very next verse St Paul states that "not all flesh [σάρξ] is alike, but there is one kind for men, another for animals, another for birds, and another for fish" (15:39). We may notice a certain distinction in the use of these terms in 1 Corinthians 15.

The human being is "body" or "flesh." When we speak of the body, we are often referring to a part of our total being, but when St Paul uses "body" he means the whole person seen from one particular angle: in a particular relationship to God. The term "flesh" also stands for the whole man, but man as a weak creature alienated and separated from God. The concept of "body" refers both to earthly and heavenly realities, while the concept of "flesh" only to the earthly.[6]

When St Paul refers to man as flesh, he has in mind man under the power of the corruptive forces of death. Sin is not being in flesh, but living according to the flesh. The works or fruits of this type of living, as enumerated in another of St Paul's epistles, are "immorality, impurity, licentiousness, idolatry, sorcery, enmity, strife, jealousy, anger, selfishness, dissension, party spirit, envy, drunkenness, carousing, and the like" (Ga 5:19-21). We can see from this list that "flesh" in St Paul's view points beyond sheer physicality—it refers to the totality of man, not only to his physical but also to his mental and psychological aspects.[7] Man as flesh is "unspiri-

---

[6]Robert H. Gundry, *Soma in Biblical Theology with Emphasis on Pauline Anthropology* (Cambridge: University Press, 1976) 161-9.

[7]M. E. Dahl, *The Resurrection of the Body: A Study of I Corinthians 15,*

tual," for "those who live according to the flesh set their minds
on the things of the flesh," and "the mind that is set on the
flesh is hostile to God" (Rm 8:5, 7). On the other hand, man
as "spirit" is not man without body or flesh, but man who is
open to and guided by the Spirit, who produces the "fruit of
the Spirit"—which is "love, joy, peace, patience, kindness,
goodness, faithfulness, gentleness, self-control; against
[which] there is no law" (Ga 5:22-23). All three terms—
body, flesh and spirit—in their predominant Pauline usage
specify man as a whole, in his various relations to God.[8]

The Influence of Philosophy on Exegesis

Some modern lines of interpretation of the Pauline an-
thropological terminology of "body" and "flesh" betray the
heavy influence of twentieth-century philosophical considera-
tions. The existentialist philosophy of our century has influenced some modern theologians and exegetes to see Pauline
anthropology primarily in terms of a concept of relationship.
"Man is a being who has a relationship to himself," in the
words of Rudolf Bultmann, and this relationship can be
"either an appropriate or a perverted one," meaning that "he
can be at one with himself or at odds; . . . he can be under his
own control or lose his grip on himself."[9]

Exegetical trends influenced by existentialism have little

Studies in Biblical Theology, 1st series, 36 (London: SCM Press, 1962) 121.

Paul's use of the term "body" does not always correspond to this predominant usage. The term may also refer "simply to the body of Christ's
flesh, the human, material body that experienced death on the cross, or to any
other human body." See C. K. Barrett, *From First Adam to Last: A Study in
Pauline Theology* (London: Adam and Charles Black, 1962) 96. See also
J. A. T. Robinson, *The Body: A Study in Pauline Theology,* Studies in Biblical
Theology, 1st series, 5 (London: SCM Press, 1952).

[8]In addition to this predominant conception of body or flesh, St Paul also
expressed another one, in which this earthly flesh or body is seen as "the
temporary receptacle of the soul," which indwells and rules, and separates
itself from the body at death (Ph 1:22-24). See J. H. Houlden, *Paul's Letters
from Prison,* Pelican New Testament Commentaries (Baltimore: Penguin
Books, 1970) 63.

[9]Rudolf Bultmann, *Theology of the New Testament,* 2 vols. (New York:
Charles Scribner's Sons, 1951) 1:197f, 202f.

to do with St Paul's actual views. The meaning of Paul's terminology simply cannot be fully conveyed when man as body, man in his wholeness, embracing both body and soul, is reduced to the concept of self-understanding. The idea that man as σῶμα can separate from himself and come under the dominance of outside powers is not something that is contrary to Paul's thought, but it is only one aspect of his total vision of man. Paul thinks of man primarily in relation to God and Christ, not in relation to himself. The existentialists reduce Paul's theocentric and Christocentric vision to an anthropocentric one.

Throughout history current philosophical insights have been used in the service of the gospel, following the example of the early Church, which made use of Hellenistic concepts and language. However, these concepts and terminologies were transformed and Christianized in the contexts in which they were employed. What characterizes many modern attempts to understand σῶμα and σάρξ is not the transformation of philosophical concepts, but quite the opposite: the transmutation of the very core of the gospel message. Many existentialists undoubtedly act out of a pastoral concern, attempting to make the bodily resurrection of Christ easily understandable to the mind of modern man. After all, if the "body" in St Paul can be interpreted only in terms of self-understanding, then the resurrection of the "body" would no longer stand as a "scandal" to modern intelligence. The results of this approach, however, are quite clear: the actual New Testament witness to the bodily resurrection is sacrificed to current modes of thought.[10]

We would like to stress once more that when Paul writes about the bodies that will be resurrected he has in mind the resurrection of man as a whole, body and soul together. As the second-century Christian apologist Athenagoras expresses it in his treatise *On the Resurrection of the Dead:*

God gave independent being and life neither to the nature of the soul by itself, nor to the nature of the

[10]See Gundry, 161-9.

body separately, but rather to men, composed of soul
and body, so that with these same parts of which they
are composed, when they are born and live, they should
attain after the termination of this life their common
end; soul and body compose in man *one living entity.*

After quoting this passage, Georges Florovsky comments
that the basic presupposition of this early Christian writer's
argument is that man without body would no longer be a
man—the identity of the individual would be destroyed. Without the bodily resurrection, man as man would cease to exist,
for the body belongs to the fulness of human existence.[11]

"Flesh and Blood Cannot Inherit the Kingdom"

The flesh in itself is not evil. Yet when St Paul deals
with the resurrection he uses the term "body"—not "flesh."
And he writes about a "spiritual body," but never about a
"spiritual flesh." He even asserts that "flesh and blood cannot
inherit the kingdom of God" (1 Cor 15:50). This was a
favorite passage of the gnostics, who took it as confirmation
of their interpretation of spiritual resurrection, "the illumination of the mind by the truth."[12] In their view, flesh would be
excluded from the kingdom of God and could not be saved.

This attitude was vigorously opposed by the early fathers
of the Church, who warned that with this interpretation the
gnostics overturned God's entire plan for man's salvation,
which is the resurrection of the body. St Irenaeus pointed out
that if the resurrection is only spiritual, then the created
world, "the handiwork of God," is not saved. When St Paul
says that flesh and blood cannot inherit the kingdom, St
Irenaeus argues that he is speaking of the weaknesses of the
flesh, the "works" of the flesh, not flesh as such.[13] Man as

[11]Georges Florovsky, *Creation and Redemption,* Collected Works, 3 (Belmont, Mass.: Nordland, 1976) 221-2.

[12]J. N. D. Kelly, *Early Christian Doctrines,* rev. ed. (New York: Harper
& Row, 1978) 467.

[13]Irenaeus, *Against Heresies* 5:13:2-3, in A. Roberts, J. Donaldson and

flesh cannot enter the kingdom, yet flesh, the material substance, the body in itself, can be transformed and brought
under the rule and power of the Spirit. Flesh is capable of
corruption, but also of incorruption. Since "the Word became
flesh [σὰρξ]" (Jn 1:14), it could also receive the life which
flows from Christ, it was also healed by him. Again, according to St Irenaeus, "the final result of the work of the Spirit
is the salvation of the flesh." It is true that "flesh cannot by
itself possess the kingdom of God by inheritance; but it can
be taken *for* an inheritance into the kingdom of God."[14]

Tertullian, in commenting on 1 Corinthians 15:50, agreed
that "the works of the flesh and blood"—enumerated in Galatians 5:19-21—"deprive men of the Kingdom of God." The
kingdom is denied to the works of the flesh, but "not to the
substance thereof. For not that is condemned in which evil
is done, but only the evil which is done in it. The flesh will
rise, and when changed it will obtain the kingdom."[15] The
author of the anonymous sermon commonly called the *Second
Letter to the Corinthians* and ascribed to St Clement of Rome,
writes:

> Moreover, let none of you say that this flesh will not
> be judged or rise again. Consider this: In what state
> were you saved? In what state did you regain your
> sight, if it was not while you were in this flesh? There-
> fore, we should guard the flesh as God's temple. For
> just as you were called in the flesh, you will come in
> the flesh. If Christ the Lord who saved us was made
> flesh though he was at first spirit, and called us in this
> way, in the same way we too in this very flesh will
> receive our reward.[16]

Resurrection could not be only spiritual or a transformation
of the human personality, but it must be a transformation of

A. C. Coxe, eds., *Ante-Nicene Fathers* [ANF], 10 vols. (New York, 1885-
1897) 1:540.

[14]Ibid., 538 (5:12:4) and 535 (5:9:4).

[15]Tertullian, *Against Marcion*, in ANF 3:451.

[16]Cyril C. Richardson, ed., *Early Christian Fathers*, Library of Christian
Classics, 1 (Philadelphia: Westminster Press, 1953) 196.

the body too, of the whole man. At the resurrection all is transformed by the power of God.

C.F.D. Moule, in his article "St. Paul and Dualism," has developed the thesis that the apostle taught neither a materialistic doctrine of physical resurrection nor a dualistic doctrine of the escape of the soul from the body. Paul does not say that the body, flesh or matter is to be preserved just as it is, but is to be "transformed into that which transcends it." The possibility of a complete and ultimate transformation of the body Paul relates to God's triumphant act of conquest in raising Christ from among the dead (Rm 6:4; 1 Cor 15:26f). Moule stresses throughout this important article that Paul has no use for any antithesis between spirit and matter. The only dualism that he is interested in is a "moral dualism" of obedience and disobedience. For Paul, "man's predicament is not that he is ἐν σαρκί [in flesh] but that, *via* his σάρξ, sin has got hold of him." Man's destiny is seen in terms of a transformation of the body and not in terms of a disembodied soul. It is the Spirit of God who cooperates with man in producing "the deeds and words of filial obedience" and effects the transformation of the body which has already begun and which will be completed at the time of the parousia (Rm 8:23f; 1 Cor 15:23; Ph 3:20f; Col 3:4; 1 Th 4:15f). Matter, the body, is important and is transformed in the process of surrender to God's will. Paul believes in the transformation by God, because God by his power raised up Christ and is also able to raise our mortal bodies (Rm 8:11).[17]

The early Christian teachers and theologians who fought the gnostics and what they called "their folly" saw the flesh (σάρξ) as potentially a vehicle for the glory of God, and they understood Paul's negative evaluation of flesh as referring to flesh in its evil action, not to flesh as material substance. Chrysostom interpreted 1 Corinthians 15:50 in a moral sense, as "men's evil deeds." The fathers in general interpreted Paul's warning against "flesh" to mean that flesh

[17]C. F. D. Moule, "St. Paul and Dualism: The Pauline Conception of Resurrection," *New Testament Studies* 12:2 (1966) 106-23, especially 107, 113-5.

would be restored to its proper place only if it was related to God and subordinated to the Spirit.[18]

The concluding words of St Paul in 1 Corinthians 15:50, that neither does "the perishable [ἡ φθορά] inherit the imperishable [τὴν ἀφθαρσίαν]," indicate once again that this verse is not referring to material substance but to the evil works of the flesh. St John Chrysostom notes that "if he were speaking of the body and not of evil doing he would not have said 'corruption.' For [Paul] nowhere calls the body 'corruption,' since neither is it corruption, but a thing corruptible."[19] To remove any misunderstanding about this matter, the apostle goes on to write that what is corruptible (τὸ φθαρτὸν) must put on incorruption (ἀφθαρσίαν, 1 Cor 15:53). The body is not identified with corruption. Death and corruption are consequences of sin.

This biblical view of the body, death and corruption is summarized and expressed with force and clarity by Chrysostom in the following manner:

> The body is one thing, corruption another . . . the body is corruptible but is not corruption; the body is mortal, but is not death. Rather is the body a work of God while corruption and death, on the other hand, first came into being through sin. That which is foreign to me, says Paul, that I desire to cast off, not that which is my own. What is foreign to us, however, is not the body but corruptibility.[20]

For this father of the Church, what is abolished in the resurrection is corruption, but not the body. At the resurrection

---

[18]See Maurice F. Wiles, *The Divine Apostle: Interpretation of St. Paul's Epistles in the Early Church* (Cambridge: University Press, 1967) 26-7. The fathers saw a moral significance in 1 Cor 15:50. No doubt this interpretation contains "a true and important insight." Yet if "it is applied too automatically . . . it can give rise to serious misinterpretation of [Paul's] meaning in many cases" (29).

[19]*Homilies on Acts* 42, NPNF 11:256.

[20]*On the Resurrection of the Dead,* quoted in Nicholas Arseniev, *Mysticism and the Eastern Church* (Crestwood, N.Y.: SVS Press, 1979) 27f; and in Georges Florovsky, "The Gospel of Resurrection (I Cor. 15)," in *Paulus-Hellas-Oikoumene: An Ecumenical Symposium* (Athens, 1951) 74.

man will finally be free from foreign, unnatural elements that
cling to the body. The body will be resurrected and corruption and death will be eliminated by the power of God. Then
the final destiny of mankind will be realized, and in the new
life death and corruption will no longer have dominion over
men. There will be no resistance to the appeals of the Spirit
of God. Wherever the Spirit moves, the new transformed
body will follow in perfect harmony with it. What is perishable will now be raised as imperishable and glorious. The
weak will be raised as powerful, the slave as finally free.

At the Matins of Holy Saturday, the Church announces
the resurrection with the words: "By death dost Thou transform mortality, and by Thy burial, corruption," and "that
which was corruptible in Thy human nature Thou hast transformed to incorruption, and by Thy Resurrection Thou hast
revealed a fountain of immortal life."[21] How are we to understand the words of this hymn, that "that which was corruptible
in Thy human nature Thou hast transformed"? What was
corruptible in Christ? Before the resurrection the body of
Christ was liable to hunger, thirst, weariness and death itself.
This is one meaning of the word "corruption," according to
St John of Damascus, who summarized the teaching of the
fathers. But the real meaning of the term is corruption as the
decomposition of the body. The Holy One did not see corruption (Acts 2:27), his body never became a corpse. In this
sense his body was incorruptible.[22] Death had no dominion
over him. St Cyril of Alexandria maintains that the flesh,
united to the lifegiving Word, is raised to the power of the
Word. "Of all other men it is true that 'the flesh profiteth
nothing'; of Christ alone it is not true, since in His flesh
dwells Life . . . the only-begotten Son."[23]

---

[21]Canon of Matins of Holy Saturday, verses on odes 5 and 6, in Mother
Mary and Archimandrite Kallistos Ware, trs. and eds., *Lenten Triodion* (London: Faber and Faber, 1978) 648f.

[22]Georges Florovsky, "On the Tree of the Cross," *St. Vladimir's Seminary
Quarterly* 1:3-4 (1953) 19.

[23]*In Joh.*, 4, cited in Emile Mersch, *The Whole Christ: The Historical
Development of the Doctrine of the Mystical Body in Scripture and Tradition*
(Milwaukee: Bruce Co., 1938) 339-41.

Life after Death

Man as a body means man as a living being, man as a whole. Being body, he is able to communicate with others. A man who lives "in Christ" and dies "in Christ," according to the teaching of the apostle Paul, will continue to belong to the body of Christ. "For we know that if the earthly tent we live in is destroyed, we have a building from God, a house not made with hands, eternal in the heavens" (2 Cor 5:1). This verse is crucial for an understanding of Paul's view of life after death, which he gives in 2 Corinthians 4:16-5:10. He does not write "we hope" but "we know." The Christian hope of the future is linked with the knowledge of what God did in the past and what he is doing in the present for the salvation of mankind. Christian hope is rooted in the conviction that the divine act of salvation was accomplished in the life, death and resurrection of Christ.[24] Therefore, man "in Christ" looks toward the future with trust and patience while he awaits its realization. St Paul expresses the strength of the Christian conviction and the assurance that Christian expectations will be realized.

At the moment of death, Paul writes, we possess a "building" provided by God. The building referred to here is probably the body of Christ, into which we were incorporated at the time of our baptism. The Church is also described as a building in 1 Corinthians 3:10, and in 1 Corinthians 12:27 the Christian community is described as the body of Christ, of which we are all members. Christians have courage and confidence because they are not left alone in the life after death. The relationship to Christ that is established in baptism is not destroyed by physical death, but continues after death—there is no end to it. What started on earth goes on uninterrupted in heaven. Thus, the fear of loneliness is overcome.[25]

[24]Gerhard Kittel, ed., *Theological Dictionary of the New Testament,* 10 vols. (Grand Rapids, Mich.: Eerdmans, 1964-1976) 2:532.

[25]See an interesting discussion and clearly expressed view on this point in Margaret E. Thrall, *I and II Corinthians,* Cambridge Biblical Commentary (Cambridge: University Press, 1965) 145ff. For Paul the body is not some-

As members of the Christian community, those who fall asleep before the general resurrection need not fear that the soul separated from the body will live a ghostly existence alone in space, for it is embodied "in Christ." Those who live "in Christ," that is, those who are incorporated in him, share already by anticipation in the glory of the end of time. Here we see a most profound difference between Paul's vision of the life that follows death, on the one hand, and the Old Testament concept of Sheol and the Greek idea of death as sleep, on the other. Christians who are fallen asleep are fallen asleep "in Christ" and have not perished (1 Cor 15:18), for Christ has been raised from the dead.[26] Rather they are "clothed," for they are "at home with the Lord" (2 Cor 5:8). "For to me to live is Christ, and to die is gain," writes St Paul to the Philippians, and "My desire is to depart and be with Christ, for that is far better" (1:21, 23-24).

After his conversion, Paul could no longer profess the sharp division between this age and the age to come to which rabbinic Judaism adhered. With the resurrection of Christ, the glory of the age to come has already been inaugurated. Paul had died and risen with Christ, and he now saw those things that belong to the future in a new light, on the basis of a new experience. He refers to life after death in terms of our corporate life in Christ. "None of us lives to himself, and none of us dies to himself. If we live, we live to the Lord, and if we die, we die to the Lord; so then, whether we live or whether we die, we are the Lord's. For to this end Christ died and lived again, that he might be Lord both of the dead and of the living" (Rm 14:7-9).

Neither Paul nor any of the other New Testament writers taught that resurrection would immediately follow the moment of each individual death. The resurrection will occur at Christ's second coming, the parousia, for all at the same time. When Christ appears for the final time, those who are

thing that separates one individual from another, but rather is the "means of union with others."

[26]"This is the prime theological conviction and it is seen as the common factor in all modes of Christian existence." Houlden, 62.

in him will also appear with him in glory (Col 3:4), with resurrected bodies.[27]

"Sowing and Harvesting" and "Celestial Bodies"

This leads us back to the questions of the Corinthians: "How are the dead raised? With what kind of body do they come?" (1 Cor 15:35) In response, Paul uses an analogy taken from natural life, the analogy of a seed: "What you sow does not come to life unless it dies. And what you sow is not the body which is to be, but a bare kernel, perhaps of wheat or of some other grain. But God gives it a body as he has chosen, and to each kind of seed its own body" (15:36-38).

The Christians in the Church at Corinth were well acquainted with the meaning of the images of sowing and harvesting, of the correspondence between what is sown and what is reaped. When St Paul asked them, "If we have sown spiritual good among you, is it too much if we reap your material benefits?" (1 Cor 9:11) they understood the metaphorical use of sowing and reaping. Any help that the community provided was seen as the harvest of the seed planted by Christian missionaries. This imagery is also used by St Paul elsewhere (2 Cor 9:10; Ga 6:8), and probably had a place in the most primitive Christian instruction and proclamation, according to Harold Riesenfeld. Jesus himself used it before the Christian missionaries did, in reference to his own death and resurrection: "Truly, truly I say to you, unless a grain of

---

[27]Paul does not apparently address the question of non-Christians in 1 and 2 Corinthians, although the general judgment mentioned in 1 Cor 15:24ff presumably includes them. See Lucien Cerfaux, *Christ in the Theology of St. Paul* (New York: Herder and Herder, 1959) 51. General resurrection may be implied also in the resurrection of Christians, for any theory of a millenium, of an earthly reign of Christ coming after the parousia but before the end of time, is foreign to St Paul and does not fit with his theology. He is not interested in an earthly kingdom of Christ. In 1 Th 4:13ff "the parousia ends with the judgment"; in 2 Th 2 "the parousia ends with the annihilation of anti-Christ and the whole power of sin" (51-2, n 57). Acts 24:15 speaks of the resurrection of both the just and the unjust, and Rm 2:5ff about God's righteous judgment for all, the Jews and the Greeks.

wheat falls into the earth and dies, it remains alone; but if it dies, it bears much fruit" (Jn 12:24).

Riesenfeld has convincingly argued that the words "unless a grain of wheat dies" are central to both John 12:24 and 1 Corinthians 15:36, only in the Gospel of St John they are used Christologically, whereas in St Paul's letter to the Corinthians they are applied to the ultimate destiny of Christians.[28] These two texts are related, and both support Paul's main argument in 1 Corinthians 15, which is that the general resurrection of the future depends upon the death and resurrection of Christ. "If Christ has not been raised, your faith is futile and you are still in your sins" (1 Cor 15:17). At the end, God will reap the harvest, but Christ already is "the first fruits of those who have fallen asleep" (1 Cor 15:20). He is the beginning, and the beginning corresponds to the end.[29]

From the analogy of the seed, Paul turns to one of celestial bodies. "There are celestial bodies and there are terrestrial bodies; but the glory of the celestial is one, and the glory of the terrestrial is another. There is one glory of the sun, and another glory of the moon, and another glory of the stars" (1 Cor 15:40-41). The resurrected body that will be given in the future, which St Paul compares in its glory to a star or sun, recalls its description in Judaic tradition "as possessing a glory which would equal or excel that of angels and/or heavenly bodies."[30] In rabbinic theology Adam is presented as being superior to the angels—not only to the evil ones but also to the good, for Adam was created as a bodily, corporeal being, whereas angels are noncorporeal beings, without a body. This is also reflected in 1 Corinthians 6:2-3, where, in appealing to the Christians to settle disputes among themselves without recourse to pagan courts, Paul asks: "Do you

[28]Harold Riesenfeld, "Paul's 'Grain of Wheat' Analogy and the Argument of 1 Corinthians 15," in his collection *The Gospel Tradition* (Philadelphia: Fortress Press, 1970) 180. He also writes that the "Pauline presentation of the imagery of sowing probably consists of an adaptation of the christological symbolism of the grain of wheat with reference to the death and resurrection of the Christians" (183).

[29]See Kittel, 3:132f.

[30]Robin Scroggs, *The Last Adam: A Study in Pauline Anthropology* (Philadelphia: Fortress Press, 1966) 27f, 47f, 88.

not know that the saints will judge the world? . . . Do you not know that we are to judge angels?" The saints—a common designation for Christians in the Pauline letters—will rule over the angels. Paul may well be implying here that the nature of the transformed, glorified man, the nature of the resurrected body, is superior to the nature of the angels, because human beings will receive spiritual bodies, while angels are spiritual beings without body.[31] The saints—those who are in Christ—will share in Christ's power and glory. They will participate in the judgment of the world, though they themselves will also be judged by the Lord (1 Cor 3:3).

Both analogies—of the seed and of celestial bodies—contribute to our understanding of St Paul's vision and teaching concerning the resurrected body. As soon as he finishes with celestial bodies and the glories proper to each, he returns to the image of the seed and of the harvest (1 Cor 15:42-44), which serves him well in teaching what the resurrection really is. The analogy of the seed points to the link between the resurrection of Christ and the resurrection of many in the future, between the seed that has already come to life and those that wait for the time of the harvest.

The Charismatics and the Future Resurrection

St Paul also used the image of the seed to refute his opponents in 1 Corinthians 15—the charismatics of Corinth who denied the future bodily resurrection. "Now if Christ is preached as raised from the dead, how can some of you say that there is no resurrection of the dead?" (1 Cor 15:12) Paul is arguing here with those who considered themselves "people of the Spirit," charismatics, who believed that they had already realized in their lives what Paul and the apostolic Church taught would be fulfilled only in the future. Like Hymenaeus and Philetus, "who have swerved from the truth by holding that the resurrection is past already" and are "upsetting the faith of some" (2 Tm 2:18), these Corinthians

[31]Jean Héring, *The First Epistle of St. Paul to the Corinthians* (London: Epworth Press, 1962) 3, 39f; and in particular see also Scroggs, 67-8.

were also challenging those who accepted the faith of the primitive apostolic community. They interpreted resurrection as only a mystical experience that took place at the moment of baptism. Without denying Christ's resurrection and the glorification of his body, the Corinthian charismatics denied the future resurrection from the dead and the future transformation of the bodies of the saints.

St Paul saw in their views elements that are incompatible and mutually exclusive. He pointed to their inability to perceive a connection between the resurrection of Christ and the harvest of the future, asserting that "if the dead are not raised, then Christ has not been raised" (1 Cor 15:16). To deny the resurrection of the dead in the future is to imply that Christ, who was truly dead, could not have been raised, and they themselves believed that he was raised from the dead. Human beings, St Paul argues, are in fact resurrectible.[32] The charismatics were distorting the gospel message regarding the future destiny of mankind by considering only the present experience of resurrection. But in the theology of resurrection elaborated by St Paul, there is the "already"—that which has been accomplished and experienced—and the "not yet"—that which will be consummated at the end of time. If they exclude the "not yet" of the future, then the Corinthian charismatics cannot with conviction uphold the resurrection of Christ, for his resurrection cannot be separated from the resurrection of those who belong to him. The beginning points to the end, the first fruits are a sign of the harvest to come, and the Head cannot be separated from his body. The Corinthian enthusiasts were rejecting not simply an element, an article of faith, but the very basis of the faith itself. St Paul clearly saw the consequences of their position and the distortions to which it would lead.

The fathers of the early Church agreed with St Paul in emphasizing the essential fact of the bodily resurrection, and they used 1 Corinthians 15 to defend the resurrection of the body. Tertullian, for instance, in commenting on 1 Corinthians 15:29 ("Otherwise, what do people mean by being baptized

[32]Dahl, 23.

on behalf of the dead? If the dead are not raised at all, why are people baptized on their behalf?"), wrote that Paul referred to this strange practice of baptism "on behalf of the dead" without approving it, in order that he might once more underline the bodily resurrection. To be "baptized for the dead" means, in fact, "to be baptized for the body," for "it is the *body* which becomes *dead*. What, then, shall they do who are baptized for the body, if the body rises not again?"[33]

St John Chrysostom saw the rejection of the future resurrection by the Corinthian charismatics as the first act of the "wicked demon." After having persuaded them that there is no resurrection of our bodies, the "wicked demon" would lead them to the second step, gradually persuading them and others that Christ also was not raised, and after this, in due course, he would introduce the notion that Christ "had not come, nor had done what he did."[34] Chrysostom also sees the denial of the future resurrection as leading to the denial of Christ, his incarnation, his resurrection and all his saving work.

The Transfiguration of the Body

With the analogy of the seed which dies and receives its body as it comes to life, St Paul defines the nature of the resurrected body. He uses this analogy from the world of nature not to display his interest in natural processes, but to point to the power of God, which transforms and gives life. The resurrected body no longer belongs to the realm of nature but to the higher, heavenly reality.

Like a seed placed in the earth which brings fruit in its own time, St Irenaeus observes, so also our bodies "fall into the earth and are dissolved therein [and] shall rise at the proper time." Our bodies do not have life in themselves, they do not become incorruptible through natural processes, but the

[33]Tertullian, *Against Marcion,* in ANF 3:449-50. Whatever the nature of this baptism, St Paul implies that it is pointless if there is no resurrection of the dead.

[34]*Homilies on First Corinthians* 38, NPNF 12:226.

Word of God "gives to the corruptible the gracious gift of incorruption." Irenaeus again goes on to remind us that it is God who transfigures the body, that "our survival forever comes from his greatness, not from our nature," and thus we must not "wander from the true conception of the reality of things, with reference to both God and man."[35]

Some early Christian apologists, without neglecting the power of God, introduced into their teaching on the resurrection another element that was never suggested by St Paul, an element that can be characterized as the "reasonableness" or "naturalness" of resurrection.[36] This element can be detected in the writings of St Justin the Martyr, who in his *First Apology* expressed the following view on the resurrection:

> Consider this hypothesis; if you were not such as you are, born of such parents, and someone were to show you the human seed and a picture of a man, and assure you that the one could grow into the other, would you believe it before you saw it happening? No one would dare to deny [that you wouldn't]. In the same way unbelief prevails about the resurrection of the dead because you have never seen an instance of it. . . . so consider that it is possible for human bodies, dissolved and scattered in the earth like seeds, to rise again in due time by God's decree and be clothed with incorruption.[37]

Origen, on the other hand, tended to ascribe a role to an inner principle that makes the body rise, for "as from the grain of corn an ear rises up, so in the body there lies a certain principle which is not corrupted from which the body is raised in incorruption."[38]

Generally speaking, however, despite their use of these images from the natural world, the fathers of the Church

[35]*Against Heresies,* in Richardson, 388-9.
[36]Kelly, 466.
[37]Richardson, 254.
[38]Henry Chadwick, tr. and ed., *Origen: Contra Celsum* (Cambridge: University Press, 1953) 281.

stressed the power of God in the resurrection and, like St Cyril of Jerusalem, warned those who would not believe in the resurrection that they must not "attribute to God an inability that may match your own feebleness, but rather heed his might."[39] In this they followed St Paul, who expressed the resurrectibility of the body as being due to God's omnipotence and the necessity that his plan for the salvation of man be fulfilled.[40] There is no autonomous principle in man or in nature that would inevitably lead to the resurrection of the body. There is, however, the hope of resurrection, which is based on the fact of the resurrection of Christ, whose victory over death is the guarantee of the future resurrection. His resurrection stands by itself as the most decisive and unique event in history. The transformed bodies at the end will be like his resurrected body (Ph 3:21). The physical or natural body that is planted will be raised and will be like Christ's spiritual, glorified body (1 Cor 15:44).

In the view of the eastern fathers, the resurrected, transformed body is of the same substance as the earthly body. They nevertheless saw and clearly defined the major difference between them. There is an identity, which may be characterized as a "bodily" or "somatic identity,"[41] but there are also changes, a transformation in the actual physical properties of the fleshly, bodily substance itself.[42] St Cyril of Jerusalem expresses this point quite aptly in his meditation on 1 Corinthians 15:53 ("For this perishable nature must put on the imperishable"):

For this very body will be raised up, but it will not continue to be weak, as it is now. Yet while the iden-

---

[39]*Catechetical Lectures*, in William E. Telfer, tr. and ed., *Cyril of Jerusalem and Nemesius of Emesa*, Library of Christian Classics, 4 (Philadelphia: Westminster Press, 1955) 179.

[40]Dahl, 75, n4.

[41]Ibid., 94. The identity is called "somatic identity," which means it "is not simply a matter of having the same 'personality' (conceived of in the modern sense, i.e., of a non-material something-or-other *in* a 'body'), nor simply a matter of his having the same thoughts, memories, associations, character, etc., but also of having the same 'body.' "

[42]See Chrysostom's *Homilies on First Corinthians* 41, together with a discussion on this point in Wiles, 45-6.

tical body is raised up, it will be transformed by the
putting on of incorruption, as iron exposed to fire is
made incandescent, or, rather in a manner known to the
Lord who raises up the dead. . . . So this body will be
raised up. It will not continue just as it is now, but will
be everlasting. No longer will it need food to sustain
life as it needs now. It will not need stairs to ascend
by, for it will be spiritual, and that is something won-
derful beyond anything that I am equal to describing.[43]

The same body that is buried is the body that is raised up.
The identity of the body or the human being is preserved, and
yet the whole man is transformed. The resurrection, according
to the New Testament witness and teaching as well as the
thought of the fathers of the early Church, is neither a resuscitation of the body—which would exclude any change or
transformation—nor a kind of spiritualized resurrection not
involving the body.

The early Christian writers and theologians saw clearly
the dangers of both crude literalism and a bodiless resurrection. For St John Chrysostom the body remains, but its mortality and corruption vanish when immortality and incorruption come upon it. He and others spoke about the transformation of the present body, not about the exchange of the body
that is "sown" for another, different one. The bodies rise
through the power of the Spirit, they become spiritual bodies,
and by the Spirit they possess a new kind of life which lasts
forever.[44]

This is another point that we must bring out. The resurrected bodies will never die. He who "formed man of dust
from the ground" (Gn 2:7) will also transform the decom-
posed bodies—"for they cannot die any more, because they
are equal to angels and are sons of God, being sons of the
resurrection" (Lk 20:36). When Christ appears the resurrected human beings will be like him, they "shall see him as

---

[43]*Catechetical Lectures,* in Telfer, 183-4, and n3.
[44]Irenaeus, *Against Heresies* 5:7:2, ANF 1:533.

he is" (1 Jn 3:2) and "the righteous will shine like the sun in the kingdom of their Father" (Mt 13:43).[45]

When St Paul states in 1 Corinthians 15:44 that "It is sown a physical body, it is raised a spiritual body. If there is a physical body, there is also a spiritual body," he is not referring to the soul or the spirit, St Irenaeus insists, but to the body. If our bodies are not to be transformed but only restored to the life and condition of our present existence, writes St Gregory of Nyssa, then there would really be nothing to look forward to but a life of unending calamity.[46] When St Gregory speaks about the resurrection he speaks at the same time of identity and change. How could we speak, however, about the identity of the transformed body with the present one when we know from our experience that human life is like a stream, a movement that constantly changes as it advances, and that these changes never leave us at the same stage—"how can that which is being altered be kept in any sameness?" This question regarding change follows the question of identity: "How could I recognize myself when instead of what was once myself I see someone not myself?"[47] These questions St Gregory recognized as serious objections to the possibility of future resurrection. He answers them by referring to the hope of resurrection, which has already started to affect man and his existence. On the day of resurrection it will not be someone else who will be fully transformed, but the one who has already been affected.

St Gregory then goes on to underline the power of God in the transformation of the human body. The resurrection is "the reconstitution of our nature in its original form," that is, the form of life of which God himself is the Creator.

[45]But what about the bodies of those who will not belong to this category of the "righteous"? Their bodies will correspond to their spiritual growth and holiness, according to the teaching of the fathers. They will receive their bodies corresponding to their works, for God with his righteous judgment "will render to every man according to his works" (Rm 2:6ff). All will live in immortality, but not all will live in blessedness. See Nicholas Cabasilas, *The Life in Christ* (Crestwood, N.Y.: SVS Press, 1974) 81-4.

[46]Gregory of Nyssa, *On the Soul and the Resurrection,* in P. Schaff and H. Wace, eds., *A Select Library of Nicene and Post-Nicene Fathers of the Christian Church,* 2d series, 14 vols. (New York, 1890-1900) 5:462.

[47]Ibid.

This form of life will know neither age nor infancy, neither suffering nor any bodily affliction, for these afflictions do not belong to God's creation but are associated with the arrival of evil. The divine power not only restores the body that was dissolved, "but makes great and splendid additions to it, whereby the human being is furnished in a manner still more magnificent."[48] And finally, the truth of the resurrection, in the view of this father, does not lie in arguments or in explanations of questions regarding the identity and the transformation but will be revealed at the moment when we shall all be taught the mystery of the resurrection by the very reality of it. The resurrection will be the complete manifestation of the new creation.

Two Adams, Two Humanities

The destiny of all mankind has been affected by the life, death and resurrection of Christ, whom St Paul identifies also as "the last Adam" (1 Cor 15:45). The new, second, last Adam is also a man as the first Adam was, but they belong to two very different spheres. "The first man was from the earth, a man of dust; the second man is from heaven" (1 Cor 15:47). The first Adam was created from the ground and thus was perishable; the last Adam is a "life-giving spirit" (1 Cor 15:45), whose material nature has been fully glorified and transformed.

For St Paul, the last Adam, like the first, was inclusive—his actions affected all (Rm 5:12-21; 1 Cor 15:20-22; Ph 2:7f; Hb 2:5-8).[49] Through one man sin came into the world, "and death through sin, and so death spread to all men because [ἐφ' ᾧ] all men sinned" (Rm 5:12). This verse has an interesting history of interpretation. Its translation in the Latin Vulgate text implies that all men share in a collective guilt

[48]Ibid., 466.
[49]C. F. D. Moule, *The Phenomenon of the New Testament*, Studies in Biblical Theology, 2d series, 1 (London: SCM Press, 1967) 29. "Adam and Christ are alike in this, that their actions were representative and inclusive. In this respect, Adam is 'a type (*tupos*) of the Man who was to come' (Rom. 5:14)."

for Adam's sin.[50] Several eastern fathers, however, saw it in a different light. The phrase ἐφ' ᾧ, which in all modern translations is rendered "because" or "inasmuch as," can also be understood as "on account of which," with the relative pronoun ᾧ (which) referring back to the word "death." In this case, Adam's sin brings about a universal situation of mortality, of insecurity and hopelessness, a darkening of the image with which man was created, and this situation is the origin of personal sins.[51]

However, now "Christ is risen from the dead, trampling down death by death." All men die in Adam, but through Christ, the last Adam, came salvation, forgiveness and the resurrection of the dead. "For as in Adam all die, so also in Christ shall all be made alive" (1 Cor 15:22). To be "in Adam" is to belong to the old humanity; to be "in Christ" is already to participate and taste "the goodness of the word of God and the powers of the age to come" (Hb 6:5), to share in the victory already achieved. Adam, who in St Paul is always created and fallen man,[52] is the head of the old humanity, but the risen Christ is the crown and fulfilment of God's plan for mankind. The meaning and purpose of the creation is fully revealed in him. God sent "his own Son in a body" to

[50]See John Meyendorff, *The Orthodox Church,* 3d ed. (Crestwood, N.Y.: SVS Press, 1981) 198, n10.

There are various opinions regarding the meaning of ἐφ' ᾧ in Romans 5:12. The "least convincing interpretations" of this expression are undoubtedly those that are based on the Latin translation, *in quo,* rendered into English as "in whom," according to Joseph A. Fitzmyer, the author of a commentary on Romans for the *Jerome Biblical Commentary.* If Paul had meant what is expressed in the Latin translation, "he would have written *en ho.*" See JBC 53:56.

[51]Meyendorff, *The Orthodox Church,* 198, n10. See also the same author's *Gregory Palamas*—"what we have received from Adam is *death,* not guilt" (125).

Fitzmyer, on the other hand, finds this interpretation also unsatisfactory, because, as he explains, in Romans 5:21 and 6:23 death is the result of sin, not its source. Of all the interpretations, he holds that "the best meaning is still 'because, inasmuch as,' commonly used by Greek patristic writers." See JBC 53:56.

[52]See James D. G. Dunn, "I Corinthians 15:45—Last Adam, Life-giving Spirit," in Barnabas Lindars and Stephen S. Smalley, eds., *Christ and Spirit in the New Testament* (Cambridge: University Press, 1973) 136, n 28. See also Hans Conzelmann, *I Corinthians* (Philadelphia: Fortress Press, 1975) on 1 Cor 15:22.

condemn sin (Rm 8:3 JB). Christ "emptied himself" of the glory that was his, "taking the form of a servant" or "slave," in order to live a life of perfect obedience (Ph 2:7f). Voluntarily accepting death on a cross, he died for all men so that they "might live no longer for themselves but for him who for their sake died and was raised" (2 Cor 5:15).

In the last Adam we have the perfect head and perfect beginning of the new humanity. The first Adam "became a living being" (1 Cor 15:45; cf Gn 2:7), but his life was not beyond corruption. The last Adam broke the bonds of death and rose superior to all corruption, having become a "life-giving spirit" (1 Cor 15:45).[53] St Cyril of Alexandria writes that in the second Adam, who is Christ, the human race "has as it were a new beginning and is raised to a new life and to immortality." The Spirit of renewal, the Holy Spirit, the principle of eternal life, was given to us "when Christ was glorified, that is after His resurrection, and when, after having broken the bonds of death, He rose superior to all corruption and lived again, possessing our whole nature in Himself, as man and as one of ourselves."[54]

With his resurrection Christ's work was completed but not ended. Everything is complete and perfect in him. He lives a life that belongs to the age to come, but those who are "in him" live still in an overlapping of ages—the old and the new intersect in their lives. The power of evil is active in the world, but those who are "in Christ" already share in his resurrection. Christ lived in solidarity with us and even shared

---

[53]Christ became a "life-giving spirit." He transcends the earthly order of existence, he is now free from all laws that bind those who know and live this life of earthly existence. "Now this Lord is the Spirit"—this is how St Paul in 2 Cor 3:17 sums up and expresses all that is entailed in his heavenly existence. With this statement he does not identify the risen Christ with the Holy Spirit. Christ was raised by the Spirit of God (Rm 8:11). That the Lord is the Spirit is another way for the apostle to say that Christ became at his resurrection "a life-giving spirit." The identity between Christ and the Spirit would imply a negation of his risen body. With 2 Cor 3:17 as well as 1 Cor 15:45, St Paul expresses the relation of the risen Christ to the community, the role of the risen Lord in the Church. He is the giver of the Spirit. See the discussion on this issue in F. X. Durrwell, *The Resurrection: A Biblical Study* (New York: Sheed and Ward, 1960) 99-107.

[54]*In Joh.,* 5:2, quoted in Mersch, 350.

our poverty in order that we "might become rich" (2 Cor 8:9). He became one of us that we might be one with him.[55]

The resurrection for those who "were baptized into Christ" (Ga 3:27) is a present experience. "For if we have been united with him in a death like his, we shall certainly be united with him in a resurrection like his" (Rm 6:5). This baptismal text speaks of the present experience of Christians as well as the future resurrection, when our bodies will be transformed (Ph 3:21). In a certain sense those who are baptized, who "have put on Christ" (Ga 3:27), are already risen with him (see Eph 2:6 and Col 3:1f).[56]

The period between the present experience of the resurrection and the future event is a period of possible renewal of the "inner" nature and the wasting away of the "outer" one (2 Cor 4:16). The Spirit is given and the power of the resurrection has been released and made available to those who aspire to conform to the image of Christ raised from the dead. As "we have borne the image of the man of dust," so "we shall also bear the image of the man of heaven" (1 Cor 15:49) through the power of the Spirit given by the risen Christ. Christ's life is not just an example, a pattern to be imitated, but the active power that moves and makes one share in his resurrected life. The Spirit is given to bear witness to his victory over death, and to make fully known what is accomplished in his resurrection.

---

[55]For a recent discussion of 2 Cor 8:9 and other expressions of the same idea in St Paul's writings, see Morna D. Hooker, *A Preface to Paul* (New York: Oxford University Press, 1980) 44ff.

[56]God "raised us up with him, and made us sit with him in the heavenly places in Christ Jesus," writes St Paul in Eph 2:6, and in Col 3:1 he states: "If then you have been raised with Christ, seek the things that are above, where Christ is, seated at the right hand of God." In both of these texts he uses the past tense regarding the resurrection of Christians. Yet the verbs he uses, such as "raised with" (συνήγειρεν), "seated with" (συνεκάθισεν) and "were co-raised" (συνηγέρθητε) do not indicate that the hope of future resurrection is reduced or diminished, but that the union with (σὺν) Christ and in Christ is intimately experienced in the present. Christians are able to share in the risen life of Christ. Compare these texts to the baptismal text of Rm 6:3ff.

8

"Now is the Son of Man Glorified"

The resurrection of Christ is an act of God in history, the final eschatological event. The resurrection is never presented in the New Testament as an isolated event, standing by itself. It is linked with the cross which preceded it and with the ascension and the descent of the Holy Spirit, which would follow. Just as the meaning of the cross is revealed in the resurrection, so the ascension shows us the meaning of Christ's bodily resurrection. The resurrection gives meaning and unity to the events of the past and future.

In this final chapter we shall examine the links between the resurrection of Christ and the events that followed it— the ascension and the gift of the Spirit. Our discussion will be centered on John 20 and Acts 1-2, which seem to provide two different chronologies of these events in the life of Christ and in the life of the Church. John tells us that Christ ascended and the Spirit was given on the very day of the resurrection. In the book of Acts, however, Luke relates that the Spirit descended upon the Christian community in Jerusalem fifty days after the resurrection and ten days after the ascension. Do these two accounts describe the same events differently, or do they recount different events, distinct gifts of the Spirit that occurred at different times and places? When did the ascension and the giving of the Spirit take place, according to these two evangelists, and what was their meaning?[1]

[1]Some material in this chapter was used in my article "Resurrection, Ascension and the Giving of the Spirit," *Greek Orthodox Theological Review* 25:3 (1980) 249-60.

Resurrection and Ascension: The Unified View

In the Gospel of St John we find accounts of the resurrection, the post-resurrection appearances and the giving of the Spirit, but no separate record of the ascension. According to this gospel, on the first day of the week the tomb was found empty, with only the linen cloths and the napkin lying in it. The risen Christ appeared on the same day to Mary Magdalene, whom he sent to the disciples with the message: "I am ascending to my Father and your Father, to my God and your God" (Jn 20:17), and on the evening of that same day, that is, the day of the resurrection, he came to the eleven and gave them the Holy Spirit (20:19-23). All these events happen in one single day.

St John does not give us an account of a "visible" ascension. He presents the ascension as the completion of the "hour" in which Jesus reached the Father by way of death and resurrection. The resurrection and ascension, along with the post-resurrection appearances, are thus regarded together, as events of a single whole. In the words of one modern interpreter, St John "regarded Jesus's resurrection and ascension as one single nexus of events, between which Christ's appearances were intervening events."[2] The appearance of Christ to Mary Magdalene takes place while he is ascending to the Father (Jn 20:17). For John, the whole sequence of events belongs to the mystery of Christ and cannot be separated.

St John's unified view of these events is also shared by St Paul (Ph 2:8ff and Eph 1:20), the author of the epistle to the Hebrews (1:3-4) and the author of Revelation (5:11-13), who likewise make no attempt to separate the resurrection from the ascension. They do suggest, however, that although they belong together there is a certain distinction between the resurrection and its fruits. With the resurrection Christ conquered death; with his ascension he rose to be "at the

[2]The risen Christ, "so to speak, on the way past as he was ascending to heaven, identified himself to his followers." Ulrich Wilckens, *Resurrection: Biblical Testimony to the Resurrection: An Historical Examination and Explanation* (Atlanta: John Knox Press, 1978) 73.

right hand of God," sharing with the Father in glory and in power to rule over all things. St Matthew too is not concerned with making a sharp differentiation between the resurrection and ascension. At the very end of his gospel we have an image of the exalted Son of Man who commissions the eleven disciples in Galilee: "Go therefore and make disciples of all nations, baptizing them in the name of the Father and of the Son and of the Holy Spirit . . . and lo, I am with you always, to the close of the age" (28:19-20).

Finally, the early Church held to this unified view of Christ's resurrection and glorification in its worship. In the pre-Nicene period the Ascension of Christ was not celebrated as a separate feast, but rather the Church celebrated the mystery of salvation as a whole, one mystery with several remembrances, of which the ascension was one. Boris Bobrinskoy, in his study of the "Ascension and Liturgy," states that in the pre-Nicene period "the whole of Eastertide (fifty days) was probably devoted to the common and indivisible celebration of the glorious mysteries of Christ, without special emphasis on the Ascension, but in general meditation upon the exaltation of our Savior in the Resurrection and Ascension."[3] The first evidence of a distinct Feast of the Ascension comes from the fourth-century Church of Jerusalem, which celebrated it at noon on the Mount of Olives on the day of Pentecost,[4] while the first homilies delivered on the Feast of the Ascen-

[3]Boris Bobrinskoy, "Ascension and Liturgy," *St. Vladimir's Seminary Quarterly* 3:4 (1959) 13.

[4]See P.A. van Stempvoort, "The Interpretation of the Ascension in Luke and Acts," *New Testament Studies* 5 (1958-1959) 31.

After the Ascension took its place as a separate feast in the life of the Church and was celebrated throughout the Christian world, Christians from Jerusalem used to go to celebrate it at Bethlehem, the place of Jesus' birth. Egeria, a member of a Christian community in Gaul or Spain, visited Jerusalem around 381 A.D. and attended the celebration of Ascension Day. This observant and energetic woman left us the following description: "The Fortieth Day after Easter is a Thursday. On the previous day, Wednesday, every one goes in the afternoon for the vigil service to Bethlehem, where it is held in the Church containing the cave where the Lord was born. On the next day, the Thursday which is the Fortieth Day, they have the usual service, with the presbyters and the bishop preaching sermons suitable to the place and the day; and in the evening everyone returns to Jerusalem." See John Wilkinson, *Egeria's Travels* (London: SPCK, 1971) 42 (141).

sion come from St John Chrysostom and St Gregory of Nyssa.

It seems then that the early Church celebrated the major events in Christ's life as a whole, and the celebration of the Ascension of Christ as a separate feast comes later and seems to have been instituted under the influence of the chronological sequence of Acts. We must caution, however, along with C.F.D. Moule, that "all said and done, it is questionable whether evidence of liturgical observance necessarily constitutes evidence against the first disciples' actual experience or the narrative traditions."[5]

The Forty-Day Interval

In the writings of St Luke we find two accounts of the ascension, and in both the ascension is presented as an event distinct from the resurrection. Luke's first record of the ascension is given in his gospel, when he relates that the risen Christ led the apostles from Jerusalem as far as Bethany, and "lifting up his hands he blessed them. While he blessed them he parted from them, and was carried up into heaven [καὶ ἀνεφέρετο εἰς τὸν οὐρανόν]. And they returned to Jerusalem with great joy [μετὰ χαρᾶς μεγάλης], and were continually in the temple blessing God" (24:50-53).[6] In this last chapter of Luke's gospel the account of the finding of the empty tomb, the meaning of which was interpreted by two angels, is followed by the appearance of Christ to two disciples on the road to Emmaus (24:13-35), then by his appearance to the eleven (24:36-49), and at the end by the ascension. All these events are presented as occurring on Easter Day, yet there is no doubt that St Luke draws a sharp line between the resurrection and the ascension. At the mo-

---

[5]C. F. D. Moule, "The Ascension—Acts i.9," *Expository Times* 68 (1956-1957) 206.

[6]Not all of the manuscripts of Luke contain the additional clause in 24:51 "and was carried up into heaven." The first part of this verse alone, however, is sufficient evidence that St Luke has in mind the ascension at the end of his gospel. It is quite possible that the shorter version of Lk 24:51 resulted from the efforts of some scribes to conform Luke's conclusion with the other gospels, which do not have accounts of the ascension. See the *Jerome Biblical Commentary*, 44:180.

ment of the ascension the disciples see Christ like a priest giving a blessing. But unlike Moses blessing the Israelites before his death (Dt 33), Christ blesses them as one who has overcome death. The disciples are then full of joy, for this priest is the Savior who will be with them until the end of the ages. He takes leave of them, but it is not a final leave-taking. He does not "go away." The ascension in this gospel appears as the climax of the ministry of Christ.[7]

St Luke also refers to the ascension in the preface of the book of Acts, which he addressed, as he had his gospel (Lk 1:1-4), to a certain Theophilus:

> In the first book, O Theophilus, I have dealt with all that Jesus began to do and teach, until the day when he was taken up, after he had given commandment through the Holy Spirit to the apostles whom he had chosen. To them he presented himself alive after his passion by many proofs, appearing to them during forty days, and speaking of the kingdom of God. (Acts 1:1-3)

The expression "he was taken up" is linked here with "the day," which refers to a special event. Some interpreters have seen in "he was taken up" (ἀνελήμφϑη) a reference to Luke 9:51: "When the days drew near for him to be received up [τὰς ἡμέρας ἀναλήμψεως], he set his face to go to Jerusalem." Here it is used in a general sense of being taken up, alluding to Christ's death and resurrection. Other interpreters, however, among them S. G. Wilson, argue strongly for a reference to the ascension in Acts 1:2, where "he was taken up" describes the specific event of the ascension rather than a general sequence of events. Acts 1:2 interprets what St Luke records at the end of his gospel, that the risen Christ "parted" or "withdrew" (διέστη) from his disciples (24:51). It serves as a link between the conclusion of his "first book" and the beginning of his second.[8]

[7]C. K. Barrett, *Luke the Historian in Recent Study* (Philadelphia: Fortress Press, 1970) 56.

[8]S. G. Wilson, "The Ascension: A Critique and an Interpretation," *Zeit-*

What is new in the preface of Acts and what is not reported in any other book of the New Testament is the reference to a forty-day period during which Christ appeared to his disciples and instructed them. During this period, it is implied, he came and departed, appeared and disappeared, descended and ascended. His purpose was to teach them that his relationship with them after his resurrection had gone beyond what it had been during his public ministry. During these forty days Christ by his acts and teaching was leading his followers to a new level of existence. Chrysostom stresses the importance of this period of "forty days" for those who were chosen by Christ during his earthly ministry and who had to be convinced of the fact of the resurrection. If they who were with him "needed the evidence of actual touch with the hand, and of his eating with them," what could be expected of those who were outside, the multitude, to whom the Christophany would be "a mere apparition"?[9]

As Jesus taught the twelve during his public ministry, so he also taught them during the forty-day period. He spoke about the kingdom of God before and after the resurrection. St Luke emphasizes the role of the twelve in the first chapters of Acts. The risen Christ promises them the power of the Holy Spirit, and they would be his "witnesses in Jerusalem and in all Judea and Samaria and to the end of the earth" (Acts 1:8). They are witnesses (μάρτυρες) in a special way—they are specially prepared and authorized to bear witness.[10] The gospels also recount that the risen Christ appeared not once but several times to his disciples, that he ate with them and that he taught them, but the period of forty days is without parallel in any of the gospels. What then is

---

schrift für die Neutestamentliche Wissenschaft 59 (1968) 270-1, n9.

Also the participle ἐντειλάμενος (having commanded) in Acts 1:2, which is subordinated to the verb ἀνελήμφθη (he was taken up), is another indication that Luke in Acts 1:2 is referring to Lk 24:44ff. See JBC 45:9.

[9]*Homilies on Acts* 1, NPNF 11:5.

[10]See Philippe H. Menoud, "Pendant quarante jours," in *Neotestamentica et Patristica*, Supplements to Novum Testamentum, 6 (Leiden, 1962) 148-56. By referring to the forty-day period Luke underlines the authority of the witness of the twelve.

the meaning of this number, and why has St Luke introduced it into his account in Acts?

The number forty is often found in the Bible (Ps 95:10; Ex 34:28; 1 Kg 19:8; Mt 4:2; Mk 1:13; Lk 4:2, etc.) and may be used to indicate a long period, a great distance or a limited length of time. In the book of Acts it is a "round number" with symbolic meaning—it is a typological number. This use of typology is readily seen, to take one example, in the accounts of Christ's baptism and temptation, whose significance was imparted by the typological number forty. The old Israel was led through the waters of the Red Sea to spend forty years in the wilderness. Jesus, with whom the new Israel came into existence, was baptized in the Jordan River and was led by the Spirit into the wilderness, where he was tempted for forty days. With the use of the number forty, Jesus is shown to be the fulfilment of the history of salvation, although the use of this number to stress the significance of events in Christ's life in no way reduces or denies their historical character.[11] In Acts we have the account of the new people of God, the beginning of the story of the new Israel, and Luke uses the number forty so that we do not miss the significance of Christ's encounters with the twelve after the resurrection.

By saying that the appearances of Jesus to his disciples occurred over forty days, St Luke is also indicating that the teachings of the risen Christ sank into the minds and hearts of the apostles. There is an interesting passage in rabbinic literature of the Tannaitic period (1-200 A.D.) in which the number forty is used in oral teaching: "Resh Laquish was himself in the habit of repeating his Mishna paragraph 'forty times' before presenting himself to R. Johanan."[12] This im-

[11]See my article on the importance of typology for every generation of Christians: "Biblical Studies in Orthodox Theology: A Response," *Greek Orthodox Theological Review* 17:1 (1972) 63-8. Typology is rooted in the New Testament understanding of history, and we must realize this as long as we are concerned with the meaning of the events in the life of Christ. Yet by ascribing such importance to typology, we in no sense minimize the value and enormous contribution of modern critical investigations of biblical texts.

[12]See Birger Gerhardsson, *Memory and Manuscript: Oral Tradition and Written Transmission in Rabbinic Judaism and Early Christianity* (Uppsala, 1961) 105. See also Menoud, 151.

plies that by repeating a passage "forty times" he probably committed it to memory, being sure that when he was to repeat it later nothing would be left out.[13] The disciples of Christ remembered fully what the risen Lord taught them.

The witness of those who were with him was authentic, for the risen Christ was "appearing to them during forty days" and teaching them of the kingdom of God (Acts 1:3). The risen Lord who taught his disciples for forty days also promised to send them the Holy Spirit, the Spirit of truth, who would clarify what Christ said and meant. Then the disciples would possess full understanding of his words and deeds. The Spirit would lead them in the truth already revealed in and by Christ, for all that Christ heard from the Father he had made known to them (Jn 15:15). And after they received the Spirit, the disciples were able to transmit his teaching with authority.

Christ's Ascension into Heaven

The second account of the ascension St Luke gives follows the preface of Acts (1:9ff). According to this narrative, the members of the community in Jerusalem, including the women, were witnesses to the ascension (Acts 1:14, 21f). They all looked on as Christ ascended to heaven, "and a cloud took him out of their sight" (1:9). While they were looking after him, two men in white robes—a description of angels—appeared and said: "This Jesus, who was taken up from you into heaven, will come in the same way as you saw him go into heaven" (1:11). The two angels also appear in Luke 24:4, at the empty tomb of Christ, where they are described as "two men . . . in dazzling apparel." There their role is to interpret what happened, and likewise here they convey a message: that the ascension of Christ points to the second

---

[13]The oral teachings of the great teachers were preserved by repetition and memorization. The very term *Tannaim* refers to those teachers whose method of teaching was by repetition, and the term *Mishnah* also means "repetition." For a brief but good survey of rabbinic literature see JBC 68:118ff, particularly 68:121.

coming, the parousia. After the ascension, the witnesses of this event return to Jerusalem to devote themselves to prayer (Acts 1:14).

The account of the ascension that we find in Acts is simple and straightforward. There is no attempt to embellish it or to describe the sensations of those who were looking on. It is worth noting that the expression "into heaven" (εἰς τὸν οὐρανὸν) is used no less than four times in this short narrative.[14] Christ's entry into heaven is the central point of the ascension account. Neither the disciples nor the other eyewitnesses saw the very moment of his entry into heaven—they were prevented by a cloud which "took him out of their sight" (1:9). Like the resurrection, when God raised Christ from the tomb, no one could see the very entry of the risen Christ into heaven. And like in the resurrection, at the ascension Christ was vindicated, God declared him innocent, sinless, and his glorified body was received by God.[15]

The ascension brings together heaven and earth. The risen Christ brings into heaven with him the human nature that he had assumed at the incarnation, now completely transformed (Eph 2:6). "We who seemed unworthy of the earth are now raised to heaven," says St John Chrysostom. "We who were unworthy of earthly dominion have been raised to the Kingdom on high, have ascended higher than heaven, have come to occupy the King's throne." After quoting these words of Chrysostom, Georges Florovsky adds that by his ascension "the Lord not only opened to man the entrance to heaven, not only appeared before the face of God on our behalf and for our sake, but likewise 'transferred man' to high places."[16] Pentecost would be the final sign of accep-

---

[14]For a detailed exegesis of Acts 1:9-11, see Ernst Haenchen, *The Acts of the Apostles* (Philadelphia: Westminster Press, 1971) 148-52.

[15]The bodily resurrection was followed by his bodily ascension. His disappearance in a cloud, which is the visible sign of the divine presence, "signifies that the end of our Lord's earthly life is the absorption of his glorified Body into the bosom of God." The mission for which he was sent by God has been accomplished with the ascension. A Monk of the Eastern Church, *The Year of Grace of the Lord* (Crestwood, N.Y.: SVS Press, 1980) 209, n41, and 199.

[16]Georges Florovsky, "And Ascended into Heaven," *St. Vladimir's Seminary Quarterly* 2:3 (1954) 26. The ascension as St Luke presents it theologically

tance and the evidence of Christ's resurrection and glorification.

If we do not find a description of the very moment of Christ's entry into heaven in our canonical books, we encounter three of them in second-century apocryphal writings. In the *Epistle of the Apostles* it is accompanied by thunder, lightning and an earthquake, and the apostles heard the voices of many angels saying "Assemble us, O priest, in the light of glory," and then Christ says "go in peace." The *Apocalypse of Peter* stresses the reactions of the onlookers, both the disciples and the angels. The *Ascension of Isaiah* describes Christ's entry into heaven in the form of a prophetic vision during Isaiah's journey through the seven heavens, and details Christ's ascent through each level of the heavens.[17] All three accounts deal with the very moment of the ascension of the physical body of Christ, which the authors of these apocryphal works could not resist the temptation of describing, going beyond given witness. The author of Acts, on the other hand, deliberately resists this temptation in his restrained narration.

In his two accounts, in his gospel and in Acts, St Luke seems to ascribe two different moments to the ascension. The gospel describes the event as taking place on the day of the resurrection, whereas Acts puts forty days between the resurrection and the ascension. In the gospel the ascension is presented as the fulfilment of the life of Christ—the final goal of his ministry is achieved. In Acts, on the other hand, the ascension is presented also as the beginning of the life of the Church.[18] Between these two events, which are separated by "forty days," the risen Christ was descending and ascending in his post-resurrection appearances. But the question still persists: when did the ascension take place according to St Luke?

To answer this question, some have found it helpful to distinguish between Christ's ascent to the Father on the day of resurrection, which was "invisible," and the ascension forty

in Acts is "by no means an isolated or exclusively Lukan idea," but "an essential Christian truth." See Moule, "Ascension," 209.

[17]Edgar Hennecke, *New Testament Apocrypha,* 2 vols. (Philadelphia: Westminster Press, 1963) 1:227; 2:682f, 662.

[18]Barrett, *Luke the Historian in Recent Study,* 56.

days later, which was "visible." It is true that many ascents of the risen Christ were "invisible"—whenever he departed from his disciples at the time of the appearances he ascended invisibly. Yet this distinction cannot profitably be applied to the two Lukan accounts, for in both cases the ascension was "visible."

The two Lukan accounts are not two different descriptions of the same event but actually two descriptions of two distinct occurrences at two different times. The ascension at the end of the forty-day period, narrated in Acts 1:9-11, is the end of Christ's post-resurrection appearances, the "last departure," as Pierre Benoit has suggested, of the already ascended Christ.[19] Any time the risen Christ appeared to his disciples and friends he had come from the Father, from the final "end" of the journey, but the leavetaking in Acts 1:9-11 is, in C.F.D. Moule's words, "described as a decisive and deliberate withdrawal from sight" and should be distinguished from simple "disappearances" such as in the Emmaus story. "It is like an acted declaration of finality. Or . . . it is an acted declaration of the opening of a new chapter."[20] This final ascension, which the Church relives annually forty days after Easter, should be distinguished from the departures during the period of the appearances. This ascension has its own distinctive character. It is the end of the privileged period of the appearances of the risen Christ, a last parting, the day of man's exaltation. On this day, St John Chrysostom underlines, "all mankind was restored to God. This day the long warfare, the prolonged estrangement, was ended," and "we who were

---

[19]See his "L'Ascension," *Revue biblique* 56 (1949) 161-203. This important article is available in English in Pierre Benoit's New Testament essays, *Jesus and the Gospel* (New York: Herder and Herder, 1973) 209-53.

For Luke, the "last departure" occurred at the end of the "forty-day" period. The post-resurrection appearances ended with the ascension, forty days after the resurrection. Paul, however, "extends" this period. His conversion, which may be dated around 33 A.D., occurred at least three years after Christ's resurrection. According to Paul's chronology, the post-resurrection appearances were brought to an end with what happened to him on the road to Damascus.

[20]Moule adds, however, that "it is a matter of finality only within a certain period, for it is expressly linked with the hope of Christ's return." "Ascension," 208.

unworthy of earthly dignity now ascend to a heavenly kingdom."[21]

The icon of the ascension, it seems, takes into account both narratives of the ascension in St Luke's writings, emphasizing the theological meaning. In the icon, Mary, the mother of Christ, is present representing the Church with the disciples. The ascended Christ is the head and the Church below represents his body. Christ is pictured as blessing his body, the Church, with his right hand, while in his left he holds a book or scroll, representing the gospel. This in turn suggests that the ascended Christ, the head, is not separated from the body. Where the head is, the body will follow. Christ, as the head of the new humanity, the new Adam, gives life to the body (Col 2:19, 1:18; Eph 4:15). Being the head, he is also the Savior of the Church (Eph 5:23). With his ascension he did not leave his Church an orphan in the world. The icon witnesses to the truth of the ascension, not only referring to the historical event but bringing out its meaning for the Church throughout the ages, as it awaits the second coming.[22]

The Giving of the Spirit in St John

With Christ's ascension, "our nature ascended" to heaven, and on Pentecost the Holy Spirit "descended on to our nature." The ascension points to Pentecost, to the fulfilment of the promise of the Spirit.

Not only do we have two distinct accounts of the ascension, but also two accounts of the giving of the Holy Spirit—one in St John's gospel and one in St Luke's Acts. Both evangelists are in agreement that the Spirit was given after Jesus ascended to the Father, but they differ as to the time and circumstances of the receiving of the Spirit.

St John tells us that on the evening of the first day of the week, that is, the day of the resurrection, Jesus came to his

[21]From his sermon on Ascension Day, in M. F. Toal, tr. and ed., *The Sunday Sermons of the Great Fathers*, 4 vols. (Chicago: Henry Regnery, 1957-1958) 2:432.

[22]See Leonid Ouspensky and Vladimir Lossky, *The Meaning of Icons* (Boston, 1952) 196-8; see also plate 6.

disciples, "breathed on them" (ἐνεφύσησεν) and said to them, "Receive the Holy Spirit" (λάβετε πνεῦμα ἅγιον, Jn 20:22). The outpouring of the Spirit here follows as a result of the glorification of Christ in his crucifixion, resurrection and ascent (Jn 7:37-39). During his public ministry Jesus possessed divine glory (Jn 1:14), but it would be fully revealed only with his death and resurrection. The Son of Man had to be lifted up (3:14), and when he is lifted up on the cross, then the people would know who he is (8:28). "Now is the Son of man glorified" (13:31)—in the hour of his passion. Only by entering into this glory can the risen Christ bestow the Spirit. The Spirit is given when his journey is ended and his goal is reached.

The account of the giving of the Spirit here recalls God's creation of man, the gift of life itself. The very term "to breath" (ἐμφυσᾶν) is also used in the Septuagint translation of the second creation story of Genesis: "Then the Lord God formed man of dust from the ground, and breathed into his nostrils the breath of life; and man became a living being" (2:7). It also appears in Ezekiel's vision of the valley of dry bones: "breathe upon these slain, that they may live" (37:9). In both Genesis 2:7 and Ezekiel 37:9 breathing is a sign of the creation of life. With the resurrection Christ becomes the source of a new creation that completes and transcends the first. According to St Paul, Christ is the lifegiving spirit (1 Cor 15:45). During his public ministry, when Jesus "appointed" the twelve he really "made" (ἐποίησεν)) them (Mk 3:14), and now on the day of resurrection he "consecrated" them "in truth" (Jn 17:19). They are now set apart for "worship" of the Father "in spirit and truth" (Jn 4:23, 24). By the power of the Spirit they are newly born, baptized, to live according to the truth revealed in Jesus.

Those to whom Christ appeared and upon whom he bestowed the Spirit are his immediate disciples. The petition of the high-priestly prayer—"Sanctify [ἁγίασον] them in the truth . . . for their sake I consecrate [ἁγιάζω] myself, that they also may be consecrated in truth [ἡγιασμένοι ἐν ἀληθείᾳ]" (Jn 17:17-19)— is now fulfilled in the giving of the Spirit, for "to sanctify," "to consecrate" or "to make holy" implies the sanctifying power of the Holy Spirit. We may regard this descent of the Spirit as the disciples' ordination, for the power of binding and loosing, of retaining and forgiving, is a priestly power, "their ordination confirmed at Pentecost."[23]

There is a relationship between John 20:23 ("If you forgive the sins of any, they are forgiven; if you retain the sins of any, they are retained") and Matthew 18:18 ("Truly, I say to you, whatever you bind on earth shall be bound in heaven, and whatever you loose on earth shall be loosed in heaven"), according to André Feuillet. This exegete points out that what is referred to in John 20:23 "is more than merely the ministry of preaching." Some have reduced the meaning of this verse precisely to this. But the passive construction used by St John here—"are forgiven" and "are retained"—is another way of designating "God as the source, just as in Matthew heaven ratifies what has been done on earth." Christ prepared the apostles for their ordination. If the washing of the feet that St John records in 13:1ff is a prelude to the apostolic consecration as priests, then the breathing of the Spirit upon them after the resurrection shows us "the complement of the priesthood."[24]

What happened on this first evening of the day of resurrection is a real giving of the first fruits (ἀπαρχή, 1 Cor 15:20) of the Spirit, according to St Cyril of Alexandria.[25] We would not be wrong, writes St John Chrysostom, in asserting that the apostles received "spiritual power and grace; not so as to raise the dead, or to work miracles, but so as to remit sins."[26]

---

[23]Sergius Boulgakoff, "The Hierarchy and the Sacraments," in Roderic Dunkerley, ed., *The Ministry and the Sacraments* (New York, 1937) 97f.

[24]André Feuillet, *The Priesthood of Christ and his Ministers* (New York: Doubleday, 1975) 167ff. Both Mt 18:18 and Jn 20:23 refer only to the apostles. They are the recipients of the power of binding and loosing (175).

[25]Quoted in Maurice F. Wiles, *The Spiritual Gospel: The Interpretation of the Fourth Gospel in the Early Church* (Cambridge: University Press, 1960) 31.

[26]*Homilies on St. John* 86, in NPNF 14:325. B. F. Wescott, in his *Commentary on the Gospel according to St. John* (London, 1882) remarks that the absence of the definite article in the Greek text before "Holy Spirit" in Jn

Christ's promise to send his disciples the Holy Spirit, made during his farewell discourse, is fulfilled on the day of his resurrection. In John 14-16 there are five passages containing the promise of the coming of the Spirit in the very near future (14:16-17; 14:26; 15:26; 16:7-11; 16:13-15). The presence of the Spirit, first of all, will be by indwelling. This is implied in Jesus' breathing on the eleven (Jn 20:22). The Spirit is invisible to physical eyes, but the fruit of the Spirit (Ga 5:22-23) witnesses to his presence. Through indwelling, the Spirit will remain with the apostles forever (14:16), and will guide them "into all truth" (16:13), that is, into the perfect understanding of Christ and his gospel. The role of the Spirit is not to add anything to the riches of Christ but to enlighten, manifest and interpret. The Spirit is the interpreter of Christ's words and deeds, the teacher and expositor of the gospel (14:26). The Spirit who is given to the apostles reveals the full meaning of Christ's words and works, without replacing him.[27] The Spirit is given on the day of resurrection to consecrate, enlighten and purify the disciples. They must experience an inner transformation to become the witnesses of his resurrection.

The Meaning of Pentecost

The second account of the giving of the Spirit we find in the book of Acts. Ten days after the ascension, on the day of Pentecost, the entire Christian community of about a hundred and twenty (Acts 1:15)—not simply the eleven as on the day of Easter—experienced the descent of the Spirit. "And they were all filled with the Holy Spirit and began to speak in other tongues, as the Spirit gave them utterance" (Acts 2:4). The early Church knew of two kinds of gifts of tongues. One is known as glossolalia, a gift of speaking in an unknown

---

20:22 (λάβετε πνεῦμα ἅγιον, "receive the Holy Spirit") means that the verse should read "receive a gift of the Holy Spirit, a spiritual power" (294).

[27]"The Spirit is sent to us by the Son, the Son is revealed to us by the Spirit. The Holy Spirit is not a substitute for Christ, but prepares us for Christ, forms him in us, makes him present in us." A Monk of the Eastern Church, 248, n7.

language that requires an interpreter in order to be comprehensible (1 Cor 14:2f). But the gift experienced on the day of Pentecost was not the gift of glossolalia but of "other tongues" (λαλεῖν ἑτέραις γλώσσαις), that is, of speaking in a foreign language which the speaker did not know before, but which the listener understands and recognizes as his own.[28] This gift of "other tongues," like some other characteristics of Pentecost, has no parallel in any accounts of post-resurrection appearances or in the account of the giving of the Spirit in John 20:22-23. The "tongues as of fire" (Acts 2:3) that rested on each of the disciples likewise belong only to Pentecost.

At the beginning of the Christian period, Pentecost was one of the major Jewish feasts, the annual celebration of the giving of the law on Mount Sinai. It was the feast of the renewal of the covenant, and also in Jewish tradition the closing feast of the Passover season. The disciples who left Jerusalem for Galilee after the resurrection returned to the holy city to celebrate the last feast of the Passover cycle. They were not prepared for the event that occurred on the first Christian Pentecost. As they did not expect the resurrection or the ascension, neither did they expect the descent of the Spirit upon them.[29]

The meaning and universality of Pentecost comes out more clearly when this event is compared with the story of the Tower of Babel (Gn 11:1-9) and the account of God's revelation on Mount Sinai (Ex 19), as well as with the rabbinic tradition surrounding these events. In contrast to the Tower of Babel, Pentecost overcomes the confusion of languages and brings the language of the Spirit, making any tongue in which the gospel is proclaimed a sacred language. On Mount Sinai

---

[28]On the problem of "other tongues" in the account of Pentecost, see Jacques Dupont, *The Salvation of Gentiles: Studies in the Acts of the Apostles* (New York: Paulist Press, 1979) 50.

[29]On Pentecost they experienced the coming of the divine power in an unexpected manner. If they expected anything on the first Pentecost after the resurrection of Christ, they would most probably have expected the vision of the Son of Man coming in clouds of glory (Mk 9:1, 13:26, 14:62; Acts 7:56), but instead they heard wind and saw tongues of fire. See James D. G. Dunn, *Jesus and the Spirit* (Philadelphia: Westminster Press, 1975) 148.

the covenant between God and his people was established. Those upon whom the Spirit descended on the day of Pentecost are called to enter into a new covenantal relationship (Acts 2:38-39). According to the rabbinic story that grew around Exodus 19, the voice of God was supposedly divided into seventy different voices, or into the tongues of all peoples, for the number seventy signifies the totality of mankind. Here, on the first Christian Pentecost, the "tongues as of fire" were distributed and rested on each one of the members of the community. Fire symbolizes the presence of God, who had descended upon Mount Sinai in fire (Ex 19:18).

Pentecost is the feast of unity, which the Holy Spirit brought about. We have allusions to Pentecost as a Christian festival already in the first century. St Paul, at the end of his third missionary journey, "was hastening to be at Jerusalem, if possible, on the day of Pentecost" (Acts 20:16). Paul desired to spend this day with the members of the Christian community in Jerusalem, for whom the first Pentecost after the resurrection of Christ had a special place in history and in their memory. This all points to the fact that the historical events underlying Acts 2:1-13 are a special, unique occurrence, separate from the giving of the Spirit only to the eleven.[30]

The icon of Pentecost in the Orthodox Church particularly witnesses to Pentecost as the feast of the Holy Spirit and of the Church. The icon, first of all, does not "copy" the text of Pentecost. Upon comparing Acts 2 with the icon, one is more struck by the contrasts than the similarities, for the icon is not a historical or literal presentation of the story of Pentecost. The narrative contains several characteristic elements, such as sound coming from heaven "like the rush of a mighty wind," tongues as of fire, bewildered, amazed and perplexed people—everybody it seems is in movement. All these essential features of the account in Acts 2 are not only missing from the icon, but what is presented seems to be directly opposed to the external signs in the written record of Pentecost. In the icon of the descent of the Holy Spirit, everything is calm

[30]Ibid., 141-2.

and orderly. The rays of tongues as of fire descend on each member of the group of the twelve, but the twelve are pictured in a sitting position, without obvious movements. Yet each one of them has his own posture, with different positions of the head, turned in various directions. Each one received the gift of the Spirit in the form of separate tongues, indicating that there is a diversity of gifts, but one and the same Spirit (1 Cor 12:4) upon whom all depend. The icon stresses the unity behind these apparently diverse elements.

This is after all the real meaning of St Luke's record of the descent of the Spirit. The Tower of Babel stands for the utter confusion of languages and utter separation of peoples, whereas Pentecost shows their unity. On the day of Pentecost, those present experienced the union of hearts and minds. They became one body, filled with the fulness of the gifts of the Holy Spirit. In the icon the twelve are seated in a semi-circle, representing the unity of the Church. The book of Acts also recounts that a large multitude was present at the descent of the Spirit. These are represented at the bottom of the icon, where a king with the inscription "Cosmos" represents all the people symbolically.[31] Thus, the icon conveys the descent of the Holy Spirit upon the Church, whose mission it is to enlighten the whole world.

Pentecost and the Church

The Spirit given at Pentecost testifies that Jesus is really risen from the dead and that personal relations with the risen Christ are possible for all. In his sermon on the first Pentecost, St Peter brings out this unity of the resurrection of Jesus with Pentecost:

> Jesus of Nazareth, a man attested to you by God with mighty works and wonders and signs which God did through him in your midst . . . This Jesus God raised up, and of that we all are witnesses. Being therefore exalted at the right hand of God, and having received

[31]See Ouspensky and Lossky, 207-9; see also plate 7.

from the Father the promise of the Holy Spirit, he has poured out this which you see and hear. (Acts 2:22, 32-33)

The testimony of the Spirit to the resurrection of Christ occupies the same position of importance as the testimony of the empty tomb and the post-resurrection appearances. God raised him up "because it was not possible for him to be held by [death]" (Acts 2:24), then "for many days he appeared to those who came up with him from Galilee to Jerusalem, who are now his witnesses to the people" (Acts 13:31), and on the concluding day of Passover, at Pentecost, by God's mighty act the entire life of the Church, inspired and guided by the Spirit, bears witness to the resurrection.

Because of Pentecost the resurrection of Christ is a present reality, not just an event that belongs to the past. "We do not say merely, 'Christ rose,' " writes Kallistos Ware, "but 'Christ is risen'—he lives *now,* for me and in me. This immediacy and personal directness in our relationship with Jesus is precisely the work of the Spirit."[32] Any transformation of human life is testimony to the resurrection of Christ and the descent of the Spirit on the day of Pentecost. God constantly creates new things and glorifies himself in his saints, in order to make it known that the Word of God became flesh, experienced death on the cross, and was raised up that we might receive the Spirit.

The resurrection of Christ is the first and decisive moment in the life of the Church, the moment which in the fourth gospel is called "the last day" (ἡ ἐσχάτη ἡμέρα, 6:39, 40, 44). The Church lives by and moves toward the resurrection through the power of the Spirit. The vision of the final consummation given in the book of Revelation—"Behold, the dwelling of God is with men. He will dwell with them, and they shall be his people, and God himself will be with them" (21:3)—may be understood only in the context of the worshiping and witnessing Christian community, for which the incarnation—"the Word became flesh and dwelt among us" (Jn

---

[32]Kallistos Ware, *The Orthodox Way* (Crestwood, N.Y.: SVS Press, 1979) 125.

1:14)—is the beginning and his resurrection the end that is already present in history. Pentecost makes it all present and gives meaning to time and history.

The giving of the Spirit on the day of Pentecost is neither the same event nor the same act of giving as was the breathing of the Spirit on the evening of the first Easter. The Spirit given at Pentecost was more than the spiritual power and grace granted to the apostles, their "ordination" or "consecration." It included all spiritual gifts, which were given to the whole body of Christ, all prophetic and charismatic gifts. The two are distinct moments of giving at two different times of one and the same Spirit. At Pentecost, the outpouring of the Spirit was for the fulfilment of the new life that is opened with the breathing of the Spirit of the risen Christ on Easter Day. And when the Church enters into the last day, this will be the consummation of Pentecost.

The Spirit was given on Pentecost for the universal proclamation of the gospel. With Pentecost the Church starts on her road of service and witness. It is of significance here that the Church calendar numbers Sundays "after Pentecost," until the arrival of the Sundays of preparation for Great Lent. This practice simply means that Pentecost is the central point, the beginning, for the Church—throughout the weeks, the years, the centuries. Everything is seen and evaluated in the light of the resurrection and Pentecost, for they are the final events in the history of salvation.

In John the giving of the Spirit is not yet followed by a public, universal mission. The apostles return to their homes in Galilee, where they take up their previous occupations (Jn 21:1-3). Their public preaching started only with Pentecost. With the first giving of the Spirit recorded in John, the messianic community was united with the glorified body of Christ. The apostles were changed—the new community was created by the breath of the Spirit of the risen Christ. In this sense the Church was born with her ministers—the community was founded with the giving of the Spirit on the first Easter evening. Yet only on Pentecost was the Church "baptized"

and given the fulness of the spiritual gifts to expand.[33]
The fruit of the resurrection, ascension and Pentecost is
the Church, where these final events of Christ's life are constantly relived and authenticated. In the worship and sacraments of the Church, their meaning is revealed, and the abid-
ing effects of the life, death and resurrection of Christ are
attested to by the members of the body. The Church continually witnesses to the truth of the incarnation, death and resurrection of Christ. The Spirit in the Church breaks new ground,
moves her "to the end of the earth" (Acts 1:8). With the
coming of the Spirit the Church is empowered to perform
greater works than those done by Christ (Jn 14:12). But
what kind of works? The Church cannot add anything to
Christ and to his perfection. All her power and strength are
derived from him. He is the head of his body. Yet Christ tells
the disciples before his passion and death that because of his
going to the Father, as a result of which the Spirit will come,
they shall be able to do greater works. Their works will not
be intrinsically greater than Christ's, but the message of the
gospel will be proclaimed to a much larger geographical area
than was the case during Christ's earthly ministry. Their works
will be numerically greater. Many more people will be incorporated into his body. Before his death and resurrection
Christ spoke about the Church's gentile mission, which would
follow his death and resurrection (Jn 12:20ff). And with the
coming of the Spirit on Pentecost the Church has become engaged in a struggle for the salvation of all mankind.

The New Testament writers fully agree that the gift of
the Spirit is the outcome of the resurrection. The risen or
ascended Christ gives or sends the Spirit.[34] The sequence of

[33]F. X. Durrwell, *The Resurrection: A Biblical Study* (New York: Sheed
and Ward, 1960) 186.

[34]It is equally true that the Father sends the Spirit (Jn 14:16, 26). The
Son sends the Spirit, but the source of the Spirit is the Father, for the Spirit
proceeds from the Father (Jn 15:26). The verb "proceed" that is used in
Jn 15:26 is ἐκπορεύομαι. When it is said that the Son "comes forth" from
the Father the verb is ἐξέρχομαι. St John consistently uses the latter verb
whenever he speaks of the Son coming forth from the Father (8:42, 13:3,
16:27f, 16:30, 17:8). The Spirit and the Son have the same and only origin.
They are two distinct persons. Their missions are not identical. Although the
Spirit had not been given because Jesus was not yet glorified (Jn 7:39), yet

events that belong to the exaltation of Christ are proleptically given in John 7:39: "for as yet the Spirit had not been given, because Jesus was not yet glorified [ἐδοξάσϑη]." The sequence of events in the life of Christ—his death, resurrection and ascension—is the way by which he was glorified. "Christ was glorified by the Passion," stresses St Gregory Nazianzen in his sermon on Pentecost, "and after he was glorified by the Resurrection, and after His Ascension, or Restoration, or whatever we ought to call it, to Heaven."[35] He upon whom the Spirit had remained during his public ministry (Jn 1:32f) bestowed the Spirit on the day of resurrection and also on the day of Pentecost. The same Spirit testifies throughout the centuries that Jesus is really risen from the dead.

"it is nowhere stated" in St John's gospel "that the Spirit 'proceeds' from the Son as he proceeds from the Father." Therefore, there is no *filioque* here. See Alan Richardson, *The Gospel according to St. John,* Torch Bible Commentary (New York: Collier, 1962) 169.

[35]*Orations* 41, in NPNF, 2d series, 7:383.

Conclusion

The resurrection of Christ is the beginning of the new creation. It is not a repetition or rejection of the old, but its fulfilment and transformation. God's act of raising Christ from the dead is a new beginning, not a return. Like the body of Christ, the old creation will be transformed for eternal life. In the case of Christ, this transformation and transfiguration is final and completed with his resurrection, and nothing can be added to make it more perfect. For those who are "in Christ," however, the transformation that has already started is not yet ended. In the mystery of baptism human beings become part of the "new creation" (2 Cor 5:17). Those who have "put on Christ" (Ga 3:27) bear the image of the second, the last Adam, and look with confidence toward the future resurrection (1 Th 4:16; 1 Cor 15:22-23).

The New Testament Church saw the resurrection of Christ as a birth into a new level of existence. St Paul explicitly connects the resurrection of Christ with the words of Psalm 2:7: "Thou art my Son, today I have begotten thee" (Acts 13:33). This new birth is free of corruption. Paul also calls the risen Christ "the first-born from the dead" (Col 1:18). The same connection between Christ's resurrection and birth also appears in the references to the death of a grain of wheat and its coming to life (Jn 12:24; 1 Cor 15:36ff).[1] The New Testament therefore sees resurrection and birth as two aspects of the same reality. Those who are incorporated into the risen body of Christ by water and the Spirit are raised with Christ (Col 2:12, 3:1) or "born anew" (Jn 3:3ff). Again, "resurrection" and "birth" are united in the mystery of baptism.

[1] See André Feuillet, *Johannine Studies* (Staten Island, N.Y.: Alba House, 1964) 266.

There are two distinct but intrinsically related births in the gospel message, one at the beginning and the other at the end of the gospels—the birth at Bethlehem and the birth from the dead. There are striking parallels between these events in the life of Christ in the gospels as well as in the Church's liturgical tradition. Both births are attended by cosmic, universal signs. The shepherds, Magi, stars and angels appear in the nativity account, and on the day of the resurrection there was a great earthquake and an angel of God descended from heaven (Mt 1-2, 28:2). When Jesus was born "all the world was enlightened," the whole creation leapt with joy, and heaven and earth were united, according to the liturgical hymns of the Feast of the Nativity. He who is identified in the infancy narratives as the son of Abraham, the son of David, the Messiah, the Savior, the Son of God is the same as he who overcame death. The account of the first birth becomes a proleptic passion narrative—the shadow of the cross is here as well, in Herod's plan to destroy him. The liturgical texts speak about the cave as the place of his birth and about his divinity shining forth from it. With the resurrection, the tomb becomes the source of new life. In the cave we have swaddling clothes, while in the tomb we have the napkin (*soudarion*) as a sign of glory. The first birth points to the second; the incarnation of the Son points to his resurrection.

The body that was assumed at birth was raised up from death. Both the incarnation and the resurrection reveal that human nature is saved. The resurrection is the completion of the incarnation. "For if the flesh were not in a position to be saved, the Word of God would in no wise have become flesh," writes St Irenaeus, faithfully expressing the view of the ancient Church.[2] The salvation of the world and the redemption that were promised are manifested in the miracle of Christ's resurrection.[3] The New Testament witnesses to this link between the incarnation and the resurrection, between the birth at the beginning and the birth at the end, and it is for this reason that the fathers of the Church always insisted on the

[2]Irenaeus, *Against Heresies* 5:14:1, in ANF 1:541.

[3]D. O. Rousseau, "Incarnation et Anthropologie en Orient et en Occident," *Irenikon* 26(1953) 366.

bodily resurrection of Christ, for they saw clearly that the incarnation is completed in the resurrection.

The resurrection of Christ is a new beginning, but it is also the end. The risen Christ is the source of the new life and also the goal to be reached. What is new in the New Testament experience is that the one who was raised is the beginning, for he has also passed through the last days. The risen Christ has made known the mystery of the future. The Christ whom the Church knows and believes in and the Christ of the parousia are the same, the resurrected and ascended Jesus of Nazareth.

Everything is realized and completed in Christ, but not yet in those who belong to him. As St Paul writes to the Christians in Ephesus, "we are to grow up in every way into him who is the head, into Christ" (4:15). Where Christ is, the body, the Church, must follow. The Church lives in and by the power of the risen Christ, and at the same time it moves toward the future, toward the full realization of him and his resurrection.[4] Then shall salvation be consummated—the new creation will be completed at the time of his parousia.

St Paul's comparison and contrast of Adam and Christ indicates that Christ is the Lord for every man and not only for those who are "in Christ."[5] It is thus the role of the Church in the world to work for the salvation of all, "to unite all things in him" (Eph 1:10), "for in him all things were created" (Col 1:16). This link between the resurrection and the world mission of the Church is quite inescapable. The risen Christ goes before his disciples to Galilee, where they will see him. He sends them to make disciples of all nations. Beginning in Jerusalem, they are to be witnesses to his resurrection, and as the Father has sent him, even so he sends them forth (Mk 16:15; Mt 28:18-20; Lk 24:46-49; Jn 20:21).

On the first day of the week, on the first morning after

[4]The relationship between the resurrection and the parousia is fully discussed in F. X. Durrwell, *The Resurrection: A Biblical Study*. Durrwell writes that the Church "is moving toward an event which historically happened before she existed, the event of Easter" (279). A movement toward the parousia is a movement toward Christ's resurrection (282).

[5]See John G. Gibbs, *Creation and Redemption: A Study in Pauline Theology* (Leiden: E. J. Brill, 1971) 135f.

the seventh day (the Sabbath), the women discovered the
tomb empty and Christ appeared to them. This is the day of
resurrection, the first day of the new creation. To mark its
transcendent character, revealed in the events that happened
on this "chosen and holy day," the early Christians started
calling it the "eighth day." So crucial was this day that they
had to name it with a name that goes beyond the accepted
notion of a seven-day week, that points to the completion of
time already in this age. The "eighth day," the first day of
the first new week, gives new meaning to all other days of the
week, of the year and of history.

The risen Christ challenges the world from beyond as well
as from within history. He ascended to the Father, yet he
"abides with his disciples forever."[6] He has promised to be
with them "always, to the close of the age" (Mt 28:20).[7] His
is the transcending presence which brings together the past
and the future. The Church "remembers" his resurrection,
which occurred in the past, and makes it present in its life
and in the life of its members. But, paradoxically, the Church
also "remembers" the future, the Christ of the parousia. In
the Liturgy of St John Chrysostom, after the words of institution of the eucharist, the priest says: "Remembering this
saving commandment and all those things which have come to
pass for us: the Cross, the Tomb, the Resurrection on the third
day, the Ascension into heaven, the Sitting at the right hand,
and the second and glorious Coming . . ." The resurrection of
Christ, in the life and mind of the Church, is not merely of
the past, and neither is the second coming only of the future.[8]

[6]Kontakion of the Feast of the Ascension.

[7]We have a vision of the risen and ascended Son of Man in the book of
Revelation, standing in the midst of seven lampstands, which are the local
churches of the world. The churches are distinct from each other, yet they are
united in the Son of Man, who is present among them. G. E. Caird points out
that it is of great importance for our understanding of the doctrine of Christ
in Revelation that the book begins with this first statement about the heavenly
Christ among his churches. "He is no absentee, who has withdrawn from earth
at his Ascension, to return only at his Parousia . . . The first characteristic of
Christ revealed to John in his vision is that he is present among the earthly
congregations of his people." G. E. Caird, *A Commentary on the Revelation
of St. John the Divine* (New York: Harper & Row, 1966) 24f.

[8]John D. Zizioulas speaks about the Church's "memory of the future" in

The Christ of the first Easter and of the parousia is the chief cornerstone of the new temple. "It is done! I am the Alpha and the Omega, the beginning and the end" (Rv 21:6). The "beginning" and the "end," the risen and ascended Christ, dwells in his body, and yet the Church with all its members patiently waits and unceasingly prays for the coming of the "Lord Jesus" and his kingdom. The new creation continues. It has begun with the Christ of the "eighth day" and points to the Christ of the parousia.

connection with the liturgy, and stresses that history can no longer be understood simply as past. See his "Apostolic Continuity and Orthodox Theology: Towards a Synthesis of Two Perspectives," *St. Vladimir's Theological Quarterly* 19:2 (1975) 83. See also the interesting comments on this aspect of the Orthodox liturgy by C. H. Dodd, in his *Parables of the Kingdom* (New York: Charles Scribner's Sons, 1961). "All through" the liturgy, Dodd notes, "the remembrance of the coming of Christ in history, and the hope of His eternal Kingdom, are inextricably bound together with the sense of His presence with His Church. The worshippers are placed within that moment at which the Kingdom of God came, and experience sacramentally its coming, both as a fact secure within the historical order and as the eternal reality whose full meaning can never be known to men on earth" (164, n1).

Appendix

EASTER HOMILY OF ST JOHN CHRYSOSTOM

Is there anyone who is devout and a lover of God?
  Come, and receive this bright, this beautiful feast of feasts!
Is there anyone who is a wise servant?
  Rejoice, as you enter into the joy of your Lord!
Is there anyone who is weary from fasting?
  Come, and receive your reward!
Is there anyone who has labored from the first hour?
  Accept today your fair wages!
Is there anyone who came after the third hour?
  Be glad, as you celebrate the feast!
Is there anyone who came after the sixth hour?
  Have no doubts, for nothing is being held back!
Is there anyone who delayed until the ninth hour?
  Come forward, without any hesitation!
Is there anyone who came up only at the eleventh hour?
  Do not be afraid because of your lateness—

For the honor and generosity of the Master is unsurpassed.
He accepts the last as well as the first;
  he gives rest to the eleventh-hour arrival as well as to the
    one who labored from the first;
  he is as merciful to the former as he is gracious to the latter;
  he shows his generosity to the one, and his kindness to the
    other;
  he honors the deed and commends the purpose.

Therefore, enter all of you into the joy of your Lord!
Both first and last, receive the reward;
   rich and poor, dance and sing together;
   continent and dissolute, honor this day;
   fasters and nonfasters, enjoy a feast today.
The table is filled, and everyone should share in the luxury;
   the calf is fatted, and no one must go away hungry.

Come, one and all, and receive the banquet of faith!
Come, one and all, and receive the riches of lovingkindness!
No one must lament his poverty,
   for a kingdom belonging to all has appeared;
no one must despair over his failings,
   for forgiveness has sprung up from the grave;
no one must fear death,
   for the death of the Savior has set us all free.

By being held in its power he extinguished it,
   and by descending into Hades he made Hades a captive.
He embittered it when it tasted his flesh.
And in anticipation of this, Isaiah exclaimed:
   "Hades was in an uproar, meeting you below."

It was in an uproar, for it was wiped out;
   it was in an uproar, for it was mocked;
   it was in an uproar, for it was vanquished;
   it was in an uproar, for it was bound in chains.
It took a body, and met up with God;
   it took earth, and came face to face with heaven;
   it took what it saw, and was struck down by what it did
     not see.

O death, where is your sting?
O Hades, where is your victory?

Christ is risen, and you are laid low;
Christ is risen, and the demons are struck down;
Christ is risen, and the angels rejoice;
Christ is risen, and life is abundant and free;
Christ is risen, and there are no dead left in the tombs!
For Christ, when he was raised from the dead, became the
   first fruits of those who have fallen asleep.
Glory to him! and power, for ever and ever. Amen.

Bibliography

Reference Works

Arndt, William F., and F. Wilbur Gingrich. *A Greek-English Lexicon of the New Testament and Other Early Christian Literature.* Chicago: University Press, 1957.

Brown, Raymond E., Joseph A. Fitzmyer, and Roland E. Murphy, eds. *Jerome Biblical Commentary.* Englewood Cliffs, N.J.: Prentice-Hall, 1968.

Buttrick, George A., ed. *The Interpreter's Dictionary of the Bible.* 4 vols. New York: Abingdon Press, 1962.

Kittel, Gerhard, ed. *Theological Dictionary of the New Testament.* 10 vols. Grand Rapids, Mich.: Eerdmans, 1964-1976.

Patristic Writings

Chadwick, Henry, tr. and ed. *Origen: Contra Celsum.* Cambridge: University Press, 1953.

A Religious of C.S.M.V., tr. and ed. *St. Athanasius: On the Incarnation.* With an Introduction by C. S. Lewis. Crestwood, N.Y.: SVS Press, 1980.

Richardson, Cyril C., ed. *Early Christian Fathers.* Library of Christian Classics, 1. Philadelphia: Westminster Press, 1953.

Roberts, A., J. Donaldson, and A. C. Coxe, eds. *Ante-Nicene Fathers.* 10 vols. New York, 1885-1897.

Schaff, Philip, ed. *A Select Library of the Nicene and Post-Nicene Fathers of the Christian Church.* 1st series. 14 vols. New York, 1887-1894.

_____, and Henry Wace, eds. *A Select Library of Nicene and Post-Nicene Fathers of the Christian Church.* 2d series. 14 vols. New York, 1890-1900.

Telfer, William E., tr. and ed. *Cyril of Jerusalem and Nemesius of Emesa.* Library of Christian Classics, 4. Philadelphia: Westminster Press, 1955.

Books

Arseniev, Nicholas. *Revelation of Life Eternal: An Introduction to the Christian Message.* Orthodox Theological Library, 2. New York: SVS Press, n.d.

—————. *Mysticism and the Eastern Church.* Crestwood, N.Y.: SVS Press, 1979.

Barrett, C. K. *From First Adam to Last: A Study in Pauline Theology.* London: Adam and Charles Black, 1962.

Barrois, Georges. *Scripture Readings in Orthodox Worship.* Crestwood, N.Y. SVS Press, 1977.

Benoit, Pierre. *The Passion and Resurrection of Jesus Christ.* New York: Herder and Herder, 1969.

Brown, Raymond E. *The Virginal Conception and Bodily Resurrection of Jesus.* New York: Paulist Press, 1973.

Bultmann, Rudolf. *Theology of the New Testament.* 2 vols. New York: Charles Scribner's Sons, 1951.

Charles, R. H. *The Apocrypha and Pseudepigrapha of the Old Testament.* 2 vols. Oxford: Clarendon Press, 1913.

Cullmann, Oscar. *Early Christian Worship.* Studies in Biblical Theology, 1st series, 10. London: SCM Press, 1953.

Dahl, M. E. *The Resurrection of the Body: A Study of I Corinthians 15.* Studies in Biblical Theology, 1st series, 36. London: SCM Press, 1962.

Davies, W. D. *Paul and Rabbinic Judaism.* New York: Harper Torchbooks, 1965.

Dodd, C. H. *According to the Scriptures: The Sub-Structure of New Testament Theology.* New York: Charles Scribner's Sons, 1953.

Dunn, James D. G. *Jesus and the Spirit.* Philadelphia: Westminster Press, 1975.

Dupont, Jacques. *The Salvation of Gentiles: Studies in the Acts of the Apostles.* New York: Paulist Press, 1979.

Durrwell, F. X. *The Resurrection: A Biblical Study.* New York: Sheed and Ward, 1960.

Evans, C. F. *Resurrection and the New Testament.* Studies in Biblical Theology, 2d series, 12. London: SCM Press, 1970.

Feuillet, André. *The Priesthood of Christ and his Ministers.* New York: Doubleday, 1975.

Florovsky, Georges. *Creation and Redemption.* Collected Works, 3. Belmont, Mass.: Nordland, 1976.

Fuller, Reginald H. *The Formation of the Resurrection Narratives.* New York: Macmillan, 1971.

Gundry, Robert H. *Soma in Biblical Theology with Emphasis on Pauline Anthropology*. Cambridge: University Press, 1976.

Hengel, Martin. *The Son of God: The Origin of Christology and the History of Jewish-Hellenistic Religion*. Philadelphia: Fortress Press, 1976.

Héring, Jean. *The First Epistle of St. Paul to the Corinthians*. London: Epworth Press, 1962.

Hennecke, Edgar. *New Testament Apocrypha*. 2 vols. Philadelphia, Westminster Press, 1963.

Jeremias, Joachim. *Jerusalem in the Time of Jesus: An Investigation into Economic and Social Conditions during the New Testament Period*. Philadelphia: Fortress Press, 1969.

_____. *New Testament Theology: The Proclamation of Jesus*. New York: Charles Scribner's Sons, 1971.

Kelly, J. N. D. *Early Christian Doctrines*. Rev. ed. New York: Harper & Row, 1978.

Léon-Dufour, Xavier. *Resurrection and the Message of Easter*. New York: Holt, Rinehart and Winston, 1975.

Martelet, Gustave. *The Risen Christ and the Eucharistic World*. New York: Seabury Press, 1976.

Marxsen, Willie. *The Resurrection of Jesus of Nazareth*. Philadelphia: Fortress Press, 1970.

Meier, John P. *The Vision of Matthew: Christ, Church and Morality in the First Gospel*. New York: Paulist Press, 1979.

Mersch, Emile. *The Whole Christ: The Historical Development of the Doctrine of the Mystical Body in Scripture and Tradition*. Milwaukee: Bruce Co., 1938.

A Monk of the Eastern Church. *Jesus: A Dialogue with the Saviour*. New York: Desclee, 1963.

_____. *The Year of Grace of the Lord: A Scriptural and Liturgical Commentary on the Calendar of the Orthodox Church*. Crestwood, N.Y.: SVS Press, 1980.

Mother Mary and Archimandrite Kallistos Ware, trs. and eds. *Lenten Triodion*. London: Faber and Faber, 1978.

Moule, C. F. D. *The Phenomenon of the New Testament: An Inquiry into the Implications of Certain Features of the New Testament*. Studies in Biblical Theology, 2d series, 1. London: SCM Press, 1967.

Nickelsburg, George W. E. *Resurrection, Immortality, and Eternal Life in Intertestamental Judaism*. Cambridge, Mass.: Harvard University Press, 1972.

Nock, Arthur D. *Conversion: The Old and New in Religion from Alexander the Great to Augustine of Hippo*. Oxford: University Press, 1952.

O'Collins, Gerald. *The Easter Jesus.* London: Darton, Longman and Todd, 1973.

Ouspensky, Leonid, and Vladimir Lossky. *The Meaning of Icons.* Boston, 1952.

Rahner, Hugo. *Greek Myth and Christian Mystery.* New York: Harper & Row, 1963.

Rigaux, Beda. *Letters of St. Paul: Modern Studies.* Chicago: Franciscan Herald Press, 1968.

Scroggs, Robin. *The Last Adam: A Study in Pauline Anthropology.* Philadelphia: Fortress Press, 1966.

Stendahl, Krister. *Paul among Jews and Gentiles.* Philadelphia: Fortress Press, 1976.

Taylor, Vincent. *The Gospel according to St. Mark.* London: Macmillan, 1959.

Ware, Kallistos. *The Orthodox Way.* Crestwood, N.Y.: SVS Press, 1979.

Wiles, Maurice F. *The Divine Apostle: Interpretation of St. Paul's Epistles in the Early Church.* Cambridge: University Press, 1967.

————. *The Spiritual Gospel: The Interpretation of the Fourth Gospel in the Early Church.* Cambridge: University Press, 1960.

Articles

Benoit, Pierre. "Ascension." In *Jesus and the Gospel,* 209-53. New York: Herder and Herder, 1973.

Bobrinskoy, Boris. "Ascension and Liturgy." *St. Vladimir's Seminary Quarterly* 3:4 (1959) 11-28.

Bultmann, Rudolf. "New Testament and Mythology." In Hans Werner Bartsch, ed., *Kerygma and Myth.* New York: Harper Torchbooks, 1961.

Campenhausen, Hans, Freiherr von. "The Event of Easter and the Empty Tomb." In *Life in the Church,* 42-89. Philadelphia: Fortress Press, 1968.

Dodd, C. H. "The Appearances of the Risen Christ: An Essay in Form-Criticism of the Gospels." In D. E. Nineham, ed., *Studies in the Gospels: Essays in Honor of R. H. Lightfoot,* 9-35. Oxford: Blackwell, 1955.

Dubarle, André-Marie. "Belief in Immortality in the Old Testament and Judaism." In P. Benoit and R. Murphy, eds., *Immortality and Resurrection,* 34-45. New York: Herder and Herder, 1970.

Dummett, Michael. "Biblical Exegesis and the Resurrection." *New Blackfriars* 58:681 (1977) 56-72.

Dunn, James D. G. "I Corinthians 15:45—Last Adam, Life-giving Spirit." In B. Lindars and S. S. Smalley, eds., *Christ and Spirit in the New Testament*, 127-41. Cambridge: University Press, 1973.

Dupont, Jacques. "The Meal at Emmaus." In J. Delorme et al., *The Eucharist in the New Testament: A Symposium*, 105-21. Baltimore: Helicon Press, 1964.

Florovsky, Georges. "On the Tree of the Cross." *St. Vladimir's Seminary Quarterly* 1:3-4 (1953) 11-34.

_____. "And Ascended into Heaven." *St. Vladimir's Seminary Quarterly* 2:3 (1954) 23-8.

_____. "The Gospel of Resurrection (I Cor. 15)." In *Paulus-Hellas-Oikoumene: An Ecumenical Symposium*, 74-9. Athens, 1951.

Geyer, Hans-Georg. "The Resurrection of Jesus Christ: A Survey of the Debate in Present Day Theology." In C.F.D. Moule, ed., *The Significance of the Message of the Resurrection for Faith in Jesus Christ*, 105-35. Studies in Biblical Theology, 2d series, 8. London: SCM Press, 1968.

Jeremias, Joachim. "The Key to Pauline Theology." *Expository Times* 76:1 (1964) 27-30.

Mánek, Jindrich. "The Apostle Paul and the Empty Tomb." *Novum Testamentum* 2 (1958) 276-80.

Menoud, Philippe H. "Revelation and Tradition: The Influence of Paul's Conversion on his Theology." *Interpretation* 7:2 (1953) 131-41.

_____. "Pendant quarante jours (Acts 1:3)." In *Neotestamentica et Patristica*, 148-56. Supplements to Novum Testamentum, 6. Leiden, 1962.

Moule, C. F. D. "St. Paul and Dualism: The Pauline Conception of Resurrection." *New Testament Studies* 12:2 (1966) 106-23.

_____. "The Ascension—Acts i.9." *Expository Times* 68 (1956-1957) 205-9.

Reiser, William E. "The Case of the Tidy Tomb: The Place of the Napkins of John 11:44 and 20:7." *Heythrop Journal* 14:1 (1973) 47-57.

Riesenfeld, Harold. "Paul's 'Grain of Wheat' Analogy and the Argument of 1 Corinthians 15." In *The Gospel Tradition*, 171-86. Philadelphia: Fortress Press, 1970.

Stählin, Gustav. "On the Third Day." *Interpretation* 10:3 (1956) 282-99.

Index of Scriptural References

OLD TESTAMENT

INTERTESTAMENTAL APOCRYPHA

NEW TESTAMENT

General Index

Abraham 83, 102-3, 178
Abu Bakr 16
Adam 51, 55, 58, 69, 113, 142, 150f, 179; second or last Adam 150f, 166, 177
Adonis 40, 44-5
ἀφίημι 60
ἀνάστασις 78
Anderson, H. 82n
angels 34n, 117, 118n, 178; at ascension 162, 164; at empty tomb 71ff, 85, 92, 158; in relation to man 142-3, 148
Antioch in Pisidia 118
Antiochus Epiphanes 28, 30
Apocalypse of Peter 164
apocalyptic experiences 57, 66, 99, 105
apocalyptic literature 28, 34
apocryphal books 31f, 89, 100, 164
apostolic mission 87, 97, 119, 157, 174; origin of, in appearances 87, 90, 99, 121, 122ff, 179
appearances 13, 16, 35, 87ff, 95ff, 105ff, 118f, 156, 158, 160, 161, 164, 165, 170; as evidence of resurrection 22, 32, 85, 128, 129, 173; bring on faith 75, 77, 99, 107, 125; denied by modern scholars 18, 21, 24; in apocryphal books 89, 100; list of 12, 21n, 78, 87, 88f, 91, 129; to James

89; to Paul 90, 98, 107, 109, 112ff, 122f; to Peter 21, 88-9, 90, 117; to women 73, 87f, 91-2, 106, 128, 180
Aristotle 39
Arndt, William F. 117n
Arseniev, Nicholas 11, 12n, 137n
ascension 59, 103, 155ff, 161ff, 170, 176; after individual appearances 106, 128, 156, 164-5; icon of 166; moment of 163, 164; timing of 155, 156ff; unity of, with resurrection 155, 167; universal effect of 36, 163, 175
Ascension, Feast of 157-8, 166n, 180n
Ascension of Isaiah 164
Asia Minor 62
astrology 39
Athanasius 39n, 50, 58
Athenagoras 133
Attis 40, 44-5
Augustine 39n, 110
Aulen, Gustaf 19n, 74n, 103n

Baals 40
Babylonian exile 29
Baldensperger, G. 64-5
baptism 41n, 99, 110n, 130, 144-5, 167; as incorporation into Christ 139, 153, 177; of Christ 161; unity with Christ's death and resurrection 62, 63, 77, 153